W9-DAY-136

MEMOIRS OF
A GLOUCESTER
FISHERMAN

R. Salve Testaverde

1986
Armand Siordia

R. SALVE TESTAVERDE

MEMOIRS OF A GLOUCESTER FISHERMAN

ROCKPORT PUBLISHERS
ROCKPORT, MASSACHUSETTS

ISBN 0-935603-08-5

©1987 by R. Salve Testaverde. All rights reserved.
Printed in the United States of America

Library of Congress Cataloging-in-Publication Data

Testaverde, R. Salve.
  Memoirs of a Gloucester fisherman.

  1. Testaverde, R. Salve. 2. Fishers--Massachusetts--
Biography. I. Title.
SH415.T47A3 1987 639'.22'0924 [B]   87-4901
ISBN 0-935-603-08-5

Cover art © 1987 by Armand Sindoni, Gloucester
Cover design by Outside Designs, Boston

I dedicate this book to Nina,
and to all my fellow fishermen,
who earn their daily bread from the sea.

CONTENTS

ACKNOWLEDGMENTS

My thanks to: Sean Murphy; Michael J. Faherty; my granddaughter Theresa for her sketches; my sons for their fishing pictures; Armand Sindoni; Josie Houde; Brad Bell; Jean Testaverde for her help with the writing; Joe Sinagra for his illustrations; Vincent and Rosie Ruggieri of Satellite Beach, Florida, for their encouragement; and to all who are part of this book.

MY TWO LOVES

I sit and daydream of my
two Loves, of long ago—
I was young and carefree, happy—
of the days spent at Sea.
My first Love, she was vast
and tempest
and of her moods, I knew
and respected every whim.
I thank her for the bountiful
daily bread she gave me—
Oh, how I loved her!
Then came my other Love,
A joyful young maiden
who captured my heart and
bore me sons so young and strong.
As years rolled by
my two Loves grew stronger
and how happy I was having two Loves!
Then came that dreadful storm that
shattered my dreams,
losing both of them to me
and today as I sit and dream
I remember my two Loves of long ago.

ONE OF THE CREW

In the fall of 1931, I quit grammar school to begin what would become a lifetime of fishing out of Gloucester. An experience occurred that year which I have never forgotten; I helped save a fellow crew member from a cruel death at sea. For the rest of my life, I would know the ocean as both provider and potential killer.

At fourteen, I was the youngest hand aboard one of two commercial fishing boats. The *Maria Concetta* was captained by Salvatore Parco, and its sister boat, the *Marianna*, by Parco's brother, Cosmo. The brothers shuffled me between the family boats whenever one was shorthanded and had use for a young but rugged boy, already with nine years' experience on deck.

The Parco boats were part of what was called the "guinea" fleet. We took no offense at our description. It hardly seemed important as we struggled to stay alive and plant the seeds of a new ethnic tradition among the Nova Scotian, Newfoundlander and Portuguese fishermen already established in Gloucester.

The "guinea" fleet was a collection of about a hundred tub trawlers: small wooden boats powered by noisy, often temperamental 24 hp Lathrop engines. Tub trawling was dominated not so much by Italian as by Sicilian immigrants; hard working, somewhat suspicious men whose blood was enriched with a thousand years of fishing tradition in the old country. The Sicilian seaports of Palermo, Messina, Marsala, Trapani, and Sciacca had sent hundreds of their sons and daughters to Boston and, later, Gloucester.

Both of my parents were Palermitan and I was born in Boston and spent my early childhood there. By the time my family moved to Gloucester, I had already fished, though only a boy, for several summers with my father. In Gloucester, I would soon prove myself to be a full-grown man.

The design of our boats was mostly makeshift. Just over forty feet in length and sitting low in the water without masts, they were hardly classic in appearance. But they were colorful, the sides painted green with red rails and yellow trim under the plumes of gray smoke from exhaust pipes. A squat cabin sat in the stern. We carried only one dory, which was lashed to the deck on the port side, and other gear. Actually, the tub trawler was little more than a traditional Sicilian dory with an engine. But it worked well for us.

Fishermen honor Saint Peter as their patron saint, and never was Saint Peter needed so desperately as when our battered tub trawlers steamed past the granite pile of Gloucester's breakwater and into the open seas beneath a veil of squawking seagulls.

Our boats were quickly rigged and manned as floating workshops. We were hungry immigrants, few even able to speak English in this new land. The opportunity to work seemed a great privilege.

Captain Cosmo Parco was my father's *compare*, an Italian word for best friend. An Italian man became a *compare* only on the occasion of serving as best man at a wedding or as godfather to the children.

No doubt it was my father's friendship with the Parco brothers that got me a job aboard the *Maria Concetta* and the *Marianna*. But it was my early training as a five-year-old aboard the family boat that kept me the job.

Tub trawling made for fast hands and strong arms. The day's work began well before dawn as ten thousand hooks attached to eight miles of trawl lines were baited and coiled into small wooden tubs, which were stowed in the fish hole. The mother boat usually reached the fishing grounds by first light. When we were ready to fish, we would carefully set the tubs on the side rails of the boat and let the lines and hooks spin out of the tubs as the motorboat chugged on. After allowing time—usually an hour—for the fish to fasten themselves to our hooks, we'd haul back our lines and begin sorting our catch; mostly cod, haddock, hake, pollack and flounder dabs.

Starting aboard the *Maria Concetta*, I was paid less than half of what the other men got. After six months of baiting hooks, cutting and gutting fish, and going out in the dories to haul back the lines, I had earned the respect of the crew. They rewarded me with a full share's pay.

Today, I can still see the surprised look on Captain Salvatore Parco's face when he realized I had hauled back nine tubs of trawls alone. The crews were only four or five men, each boat had twenty tubs of trawls. So I had done almost half the work myself.

I worked alongside my father in those days. When Captain Salvatore praised my work, my father's face beamed with pride. I had developed strength hauling trawls arm-over-arm for hours on end, day after day. Work was no problem for me; I thrived on it. I was only disappointed when the high winds kept us in port for the day.

The winds were high but not dangerous one November morning as the *Maria Concetta* fished on Jeffrey's Bank off the New Hampshire coast. Here I would play a role in saving the life of Joe Orlando.

"Joe Peep," as we called him, was hauling trawls from a dory upwind of the *Maria Concetta* when a sudden snow squall stirred up. The winds whistled by at thirty-five miles an hour. We lost sight of young Joe and his dory in a swirl of snow. As the winds continued to freshen, Captain Salvatore ordered the *Maria Concetta* to follow Joe's trawl line. Surely we would find him at the end.

It took us almost an hour to creep upwind to the end of the trawl line. We found only wind, snow, ocean and parted line, but no Joe. Unknown to us, Joe had severed his trawl line, which held us together, and now was adrift. With that wind, he had to be several miles down-range already, probably having blown right by us as we crept upwind looking for him. With zero visibility in the snow, he may have been less than a hundred feet off the deck of the *Maria Concetta* as we passed, but we will never know.

Conversation on deck fell to silence. Captain Salvatore and all the crew stood at the sides, hands gripped around the railing. Joe was only twenty-five. He was alone with a couple hundred pounds of fish and a pair of oars. Just hold on, Joe, I thought. Hold on and we'll find you.

But the snow only thickened. We were three, four, now five miles downrange from our buoys. How fast could he be pushed by this wind? We had to stop every five minutes to drop a sounding lead over the side. It was no more than a piece of lead on a length of line, which was knotted every ten fathoms. The feel of the hand as the lead touched the bottom marked our depth. Captain Salvatore kept checking the soundings to keep the search on the line of the bank where we had earlier set our trawls.

Joe Peep's father was aboard the *Maria Concetta*. He stood with Captain Salvatore and my father. Their faces were drawn. Joe's father put his face in his hands and wept. I turned my eyes back into the snow. I remembered that Joe's brother was almost lost in a dory. It was just a couple years earlier. Tony Orlando strayed from his cousin Michael's boat, the little *Pauline*. He was without food, water, even oars, for seven days. A four-masted lumber schooner picked him up more dead than alive. It was a miracle, everyone said.

Now this was happening right in front of me. Could another miracle spare Joe Peep? I kept my thoughts to myself and looked over the side.

Time passed. I could see by the captain's face that he feared the worst. Today's captains would have flipped on the radar. Joe would have shown up as a green blip. Today's fishermen don't go out in dories, and Captain Salvatore in 1931 had little more than a compass and a sounding lead.

All responsibility rested with Captain Salvatore. Whatever he said went unquestioned. If he made the wrong move, no one would ever forget how Joe Peep was lost with his poor father standing at the railing.

The snow finally gave up and left us a view of towering seas. Now everyone hung over the sides in total concentration. Great patches of storm clouds plowed about the sky, and at times the sun glowed down upon us. I climbed to the top of the pilothouse and saw a speck of sunlight reflect against something downwind.

There was something out there. I didn't dare scream out yet. I waited for the seas to roll and lift my discovery on top of a swell. "There he is!" I cried. The sun was reflecting off the dory's interior, which was painted orange for just that reason.

"I see him, I see him!" I shouted, jumping down on the deck and pointing. "There he is!"

No one saw anything.

"Are you sure? Are you sure?" The rest of the crew kept asking me as they watched with hope. Captain Salvatore kept his eye trained on the spot I had pointed out, but he saw nothing. Then he broke off our course and turned the wheel to return upwind. My sighting was being rejected. I turned savage.

"I can see Joe rowing," I hollered. "I can see him sitting and rowing into the wind. He's keeping the dory head-on into the wind." I was willing to believe God had sent that shaft of sunlight from the heavens so that I might save Joe Peep's life. I was willing to believe anything if only Captain Salvatore would turn the *Maria Concetta* downwind to pick up our lost doryman.

The crew was silent at my outburst. I could hear the boat creak as the captain looked down at me.

"If you are wrong," he said slowly, "we have lost a man." But he had recognized my determination and turned downwind.

Within two miles, we came upon Joe Peep. All the faces on deck turned happy. When we pulled Joe on deck, he was white and shaking with fright. Someone gave him a jug of wine. He would get drunk and sleep it off.

We pitched the fish from Joe's dory to the deck of the *Maria Concetta* and stowed the dory in its cradle. Upwind we found our buoys; we hauled the trawls and headed for home.

The story went around the waterfront the next day that a Boston longliner got caught in the same squall and lost two men in a dory. People shrugged their shoulders. Fishermen wanted to know when these things happened, and how, but didn't dwell on it.

Captain Salvatore told Joe Peep that I had saved his life. "Salve Testaverde saw you," he said. "He's the one who spotted you. The rest of us had given you up for lost."

Today Joe Peep is seventy-nine-years old and long retired from fishing. Joe still tells the boys on the docks that it was my eyesight that saved his life more than fifty years ago. I say God gave me extraordinary vision that day.

Many men out of Gloucester and other ports lost their lives in dories separated from the mother boat by snow, fog or winds. Sometimes an empty dory would wash up. Usually man and dory vanished without a trace. These were days of hardship. Fishermen earned meager livings while taking on tremendous risks. The dangers are still present for today's fishermen, but modern electronic equipment and bigger, steel-hulled boats make fishing safer and more profitable.

Perhaps I was born fifty years too soon.

BOSTON

I was born at home on June 12, 1917. My parents, like most people in the North End, spoke very little English, but they still managed to raise seven children in this new country. We rented a two-room apartment over an alleyway called Jessica Court in this Italian neighborhood.

On the east side of the alleyway was a bakery called Bommaderio's. I remember a macaroni factory next door to the bakery. Workmen made pasta from flour there and hung it on big racks to dry. Both places made the street smell wonderful. There was a noisy machine shop, full of motors and huge spinning wheels. Flashes of blue light came from the machine shop. I never learned what was manufactured there.

All the sounds, sights and smells of the neighborhood fascinated me at the age of four. Around the corner and past four brick tenement buildings was a cake shop run by an old Irish lady. Katie's had the best jelly doughnuts, coconut cream and Boston cream pies this side of heaven. I had—and still have—a weakness for sweet foods. At Katie's I could buy a dozen jelly doughnuts for a dime. A whole pie cost only twenty cents. Happy were the days when my mother sent me to Katie's with a couple of coins jingling in my pocket. Even today, I still can't resist the temptation of a fresh jelly doughnut.

Across the street from Katie's was a butcher shop. Whole heads of skinned beef hung on hooks in the back. Glass cases in front were filled with all kinds of beef cuts, including trays of tripe. There I would watch the men make old-fashioned Italian sausage from meat scraps. In 1921 veal cutlets sold for twenty-five cents a pound, porterhouse steak for twenty cents, and sausage for fifteen cents a pound.

Next to the butcher shop was a "skyscraper." The Hotel Sorrento was all brick and towered seven whole stories above the street. On the ground level were a cafeteria and a barroom. Sometimes I would sneak into the hotel and watch the men drink mugs of beer with their lady friends. The fancy men wore derbies and the women wore wide brimmed hats and shoes that laced up the front almost to the knee.

Past the Sorrento were fruit and vegetable stands set up on the sidewalk. I remember one man named Giuseppe standing behind one of the wooden carts, shining fruit on his apron and making neat rows of apples, pears and oranges.

Next on the block was a Greek grocery store. Against the wall were big wooden barrels filled with green and black olives. Beside the olives, there were more barrels filled with olive oil, from which people could buy either by the quart or the gallon. The Greek merchants had salami rolls hanging from hooks in the ceiling, and wheels of different cheeses displayed in a glass case. There were all kinds of spicy things and stacks of dried codfish, which my family called *bacalla*. The store smelled out of this world. I bought sandwiches of bologna, salami and cheese for a nickel.

The neighborhood bank at the corner was used mainly by the Italian immigrants. There people received telegrams from the old country.

Farther along the street were a series of food warehouses and the stables. This was the time of horse and wagon delivery, so it was not unusual to find stables in the middle of a busy market district.

Jewish men wearing long black beards and skullcaps ran the chicken and egg market. Hundreds of live chickens and rabbits were kept on display in steel cages. My mother and I would inspect all the chickens before making a selection and asking the clerk to prepare it. He'd then take the feathers off by thrusting the chicken into boiling water and passing it along in assembly-line fashion. Three pounds of dressed chicken cost forty-five cents. My mother made sure we got all the parts. She could stretch one chicken into three meals. The head, feet, heart, liver and gizzards would wind up in soup. Today I make my soup the same way.

I followed the way of life my ancestors had chosen when I became a fisherman. My father's grandfather was Rosario Testaverde, which is my name, though I've been called "Salve" since childhood. My great-grandfather went tub trawling out of the city of Palermo, working the Mediterranean Sea with hook and line, as I would later do out of Gloucester. His wife's name was Fannia; I do not know her maiden name. Rosario died at the age of ninety-two.

My father's father was born around 1850 in Palermo and probably was his father's only child. His name, too, was Rosario. He married Frances Paula Carcia, and they had four sons—Nino, Vincent, Salvatore and Giovanni (my father, who was also known as John)—and one daughter, Fannia Testaverde Ventimiglia. Auntie Fannia died in Palermo three years ago at the age of ninety-four.

My mother's family was in the export business, shipping oranges and lemons from Sicily to Naples. My grandfather was Petro Carena, who was born in Palermo. His wife, Rosalie Belmonte, also was born in Palermo. They had two sons and one daughter: Salvatore, Vincent and Rosalie, my mother, who was born in July of 1884. My mother's parents both died in Italy in 1917, the same year I was born more than three thousand miles away in America.

My father was born in July, 1882. Like his brothers, father and grandfather before him, he was a fisherman. He married my mother in Palermo in 1906, and they had three children—Pauline, Rosario and Rosalie—before coming to America.

My father was frustrated with economic conditions in Sicily. He made his first trip to America in 1910, arriving in Boston on the steamship *Indiana*. He would make two more exploratory trips before finally deciding on Boston as the new home for his family. My father came across alone and then sent for my mother and ten-year-old Pauline in 1916. My mother's departure from Sicily was bittersweet. She was leaving her parents, never to see them again, but she was also leaving the land that had claimed the lives of her two children, Rosario and Rosalie. They had died within a week of each other in an epidemic of smallpox.

My mother and Pauline booked passage on the steamship *Giuseppe Verdi*. World War I made the voyage dangerous. They finally arrived safely at Ellis Island in New York Harbor on September 4, 1916. From New York, they took the train to Boston, where they were met by my father. In her new home, my mother quickly set up housekeeping and raised a new family.

I was the first born in this country. My brother Peter was born two years later, in 1919, followed by Anthony (1920), Salvatore (1922), Vincent (1924), and Rosalie (1926). My mother gave birth to two more boys after the family moved to Gloucester, but both died within hours of birth.

Our expanding family soon moved from Jessica Court to a third-floor apartment on Moon Street, across from St. John's Catholic School and the Sacred Heart Church. We went to mass at Sacred Heart Church and all of the children were baptized there.

As hard as he tried, my father couldn't support the family alone. My mother and Pauline took jobs at the chocolate factory in Charlestown. My brothers Anthony and Salvatore, whom we called Tony and Sammy, were born while we lived on Moon Street. The family was really struggling now. We didn't feel alone. These were hard time for almost all the Italian fishermen. Our neighbors were struggling just as we were.

Sometimes I found my mother alone crying. There wasn't enough money to put food on the table and I think my mother blamed herself. As soon as I was old enough to understand our poverty, I took to the streets to sell newspapers and shine shoes. For more than sixty years I would continue to feel family responsibilities, finally letting go in 1982 when my wife died and I faced the fact that my four sons were able to care for themselves and their families. Responsibility's a hard habit to break.

As a youngster, my brother Peter developed a case of rickets in his legs. The state government people sent him away to a hospital out in the country. My mother would take my sister Pauline and me to visit. It seemed an endless trip on trolley cars and subways. When we finally arrived, I felt as if we were in a different world. There were great green lawns and trees and a little brook. Compared to the streets of the North End, this was wide-open country—something I had never experienced.

The doctors sent Peter home after two months. He wore plastic braces on his legs. He had grown so big and fat that I hardly recognized him. He looked as if he had been inflated with an air hose like a big balloon. His face had been white and pasty when he went away. Now he was fat and red in the face. Is that what the country air does to you? I wanted to stay in the streets of the city. Fortunately, Peter later completely recovered his health and eventually became the captain of a fishing boat.

Peter was not the only brother to struggle with his health. Tony almost died of a very bad case of pneumonia. I remember my mother with tears in her eyes and my father's face when the doctor said he had done all he could for Tony and now it was up to God's will. My mother was a very pious, gentle woman, not the type to argue with anyone. She suffered as her children suffered.

The whole family stayed awake for three days and nights watching my little brother's sickly, pale face as he lay in bed. The only sound from Tony was faint, hoarse breathing.

In desperation, my father put a fresh-killed pigeon, its blood still dripping, on Tony's chest. The purpose was to draw out the fever. That's what the voodoo woman had instructed my father. People still believed in a lot of crazy things, including evil spirits. On the third day, the fever left Tony's body and the doctor told my parents that he would live. My father believed until the day he died that the pigeon had saved Tony. Most Italian immigrants believed in these things, but many of the children of my generation would learn differently.

I got sick. I had the wildest dreams when I slept. I would wake up screaming, calling for help, ready to jump out of the windows three stories above the street. Luckily, my parents stopped me again and again.

In a recurring dream I would see the ceiling open up and gold coins pour out. The room filled up to my neck with coins. I would scream out, but I was to be smothered by the infernal gold coins! My parents worried about me and again they called the voodoo woman. I remember her as an old woman in brightly colored clothes. She said I had the evil spirit and, for a fee, she would rid me of it. She put a peeled clove of garlic on my belly button and a glass over it. She chanted mysterious words with her eyes closed. I lay there watching, protesting that she was nuts, but my mother stood by to prevent me from getting up. The voodoo women was called three times, but still the dreams continued. Finally, my mother gave up on her and took me to all the Catholic churches in the neighborhood. The priests said prayers and blessed me with enough holy water to get me to heaven, but still the dreams continued. Finally, my mother pronounced the Moon Street apartment haunted. She insisted that we move. We took a courtyard apartment on Clark Street, near St. Stephen's Church. Years later, a Gloucester doctor diagnosed my problem as malnutrition, and after treatment, my dreams went away.

The fishing season was very poor and my father found work ashore doing pick-and-shovel labor for the railroad company laying track outside Boston. He came home only one day a week, usually with a big sack of freshly picked apples over his shoulder. My brothers and I would run to greet him in the courtyard.

Peter and I went to St. John's School. We could roll out of bed to get to classes across the street. We had the good fortune of never being reported late. The nuns arrived at 8:30 every morning in a bus, a long car-bus with a canvas roof and celluloid windows. They came from the city of Brighton, which I didn't know at the time was actually part of Boston.

In school, I met my first chum, Serafino Favazza—"Tarzan," we called him. From grades one to four, when my family moved to Gloucester, Serafino and I were inseparable. We later fished together as crew members aboard the boat *Antonia*. Tarzan adopted Gloucester and raised his family here just as I did. He was a fishing captain and boat owner for many years before illness forced him into retirement. We remained fast friends until he died last year.

On the other side of the North End was the tree-lined Northern Avenue park and waterfront beach. All the families went swimming there on hot summer days. I learned how to get there on my own. One day, without telling my mother, I took Peter to the park and together we walked out to a large wooden raft. It was high and dry on the beach, as the tide was out. We took off our shoes and socks and played on the raft without realizing the tide was coming in. Soon the raft was drifting in Boston Harbor! Five or six people were on the raft. To this day, I insist Peter fell in and I jumped in after him, and he says he went in after me.

Either way, we both remember two big, strong hands grabbing hold of us as we struggled in six feet of water. The other people on the raft had screamed for the lifeguard after we tumbled over the side. The lifeguard plucked us out half-drowned and worked us over on the beach. The water came out of our lungs as he shook us by the ankles. A large crowd looked as he wrapped us in big towels. When we were able to speak, the lifeguard asked our names and where we lived. With the two of us on his shoulders, and a policeman in tow, the lifeguard carried us home.

I was more worried about my mother finding out we had lost our shoes and socks than about our almost drowning. I also knew my mother would be mad at me for taking Peter out on an unannounced exploration of the neighborhood. When my mother saw us on the shoulders of the lifeguard she almost fainted right there in the little courtyard. The policemen translated for my mother the lifeguard's account of what had happened. She finally composed herself and thanked the lifeguard and policeman. Punishment was confinement to the house for days. My mother told my father what happened when he came home that weekend. We moved again, this time to North Square. I always thought we moved because Peter and I almost drowned at the nearby beach.

Now we lived across from the Paul Revere House. My father liked North Square because it was near all his *compari*: the Ciaramitaro family, the LoPiccolos, the Scolas, the Molinos, the Misuracas. The families visited each other all the time, from one house to the next. Visiting was entertainment. The men would sit together, playing card games and drinking wine, while the women would swap stories and the kids played among themselves.

Although my mother believed that this new neighborhood would keep my wanderings in the city to a minimum, she found out otherwise on a sunny afternoon in March of 1924. Unknown to her, we often wandered all the way to Boston Common and to Bunker Hill in Charlestown. Sometimes with a bunch of neighborhood boys, I would take the five-cent ferry to Revere Beach or the airport in East Boston. I remember once climbing into a two-seater airplane near the landing strip. Nobody was around. My friends and I made believe we were World War I pilots shooting down Germans.

On this particular afternoon in March, my brother Peter and I pedaled a tricycle to the Public Garden. We headed for the big swan-boat pond. It had been cold all week and the pond seemed frozen over, as we crossed on our tricycle. The ice gave way and the trike, Peter and I disappeared. Our heavy overcoats weighed us down as we tried to dog-paddle. Soon, we were swallowing water and choking.

A crowd of people gathered on the nearby bridge and alerted the police. They tried to get near us, but the ice cracked under their weight, forcing a retreat. We were in the water for what seemed an eternity.

Then firemen arrived. They slid the ladder across the ice and rescued us. A big cheer came from the people on the bridge as we were plucked out of the pond. Our rescuers wrapped us in blankets and the police rushed us to the station on Boylston Street. We were brought to the basement and stood in our underwear in front of an open furnace. The police gave us hot chocolate to stop our teeth from chattering.

When we were feeling well enough to talk, they started the questions. What are your names? Where do you live? What are your parents' names?

Peter and I were starting to feel comfortable from the furnace heat and hot chocolate when my mother and Pauline appeared in the door. My poor mother was blabbering in Italian, making the sign of the cross and thanking everyone in sight. We got a ride home in the police car. My mother used to tell me I was going to send her to an early grave with my wanderings.

Luckily, my father was out fishing; otherwise, we would have gotten a good beating. My mother scolded us, but she didn't care that we had lost the trike. I think that it is still at the bottom of the pond.

Knowing how my mother felt, and with her worrying, it was fortunate that we had the Paul Revere House to offer us a way to spend our time, and also a way to earn money. I quickly took advantage of tourists by learning the words to Longfellow's poem "Paul Revere's Ride." The neighborhood kids would recite the poem to tourists, then we would pass the hat. With our earnings we bought ice cream and pizza from peddlers who had set up shop all over the neighborhood. A slice of waffle—nice and hot and coated with powdered sugar—and hot chestnuts, which warmed our hands and stomachs, cost a penny. We bought pizza for five cents from a vendor who carried a small oven on his shoulders.

We mischievously made up our own last stanza to the poem to tease the tourists and get a laugh:

And on your left
Is the Hotel Sorrento.
It has forty rooms without a bath,
Running water in every room
Every time it rains or snows.

I also learned to shine shoes, getting a nickel a shine on busy Hanover Street, and I sold the evening edition of the *Boston Daily Record*. We picked up the papers around dinnertime from a truck near the one-cent ferry. Then we dashed off to Scollay Square, where Government Center is today. While we ran along the street we'd holler out the headlines.

Sometimes my papers sold fast and I was home by nine. Other times I got home after eleven, still carrying half my papers. My poor mother would be worried sick waiting for the return of her seven-year-old son.

GLOUCESTER

I was five when my father first took me fishing. I went only during the summers until I quit school. My mother was relieved to have me off the streets of Boston. My father was relieved to have another pair of hands aboard the boat.

My father wasn't interested in American citizenship. He owned a tub trawler known only as the *703E*, but I'm sure his name wasn't on the title papers; the government prohibited boat ownership by an alien. Fishermen had ways to get around that. The result was that the few naturalized citizens among the boat owners owned a lot of paper.

Our fishing day started at three in the morning on days my father and I fished. We shoved off from Boston pier at four a.m. Trap boats sold mackerel and herring for bait and fishermen tended their weirs in Boston Harbor, near Governors Island. We tried to be loaded with bait by dawn.

The *703E* carried far fewer hooks than the tub trawlers I would later work in Gloucester. My father and I had four tubs, each with four hundred and fifty hooks. If I was fussy about handling fish and baiting hooks, I don't remember it.

Most of the time, I steered the boat while my father baited the hooks. We took a course through Shirley Cut toward Deer Island. Our fishing grounds were well inside the shipping lanes off Winthrop and Lynn. My father said the ocean bottom was hard there. Hard bottoms meant plenty of vegetation and fish. For the next sixty years I would keep adding to my mental picture of the ocean's bottom from Virginia to Nova Scotia.

After cutting the engine and anchoring the boat, my father and I went in the dory together. I rowed and he set out the trawl line, leaving a buoy at the far end. We waited an hour before he began hauling back. I worked a knife on the fish as it came aboard. An average day's catch was two thousand pounds. Once we pitchforked the fish on deck, we washed the fish with buckets of water from over the side. "Clean your fish good," my father said. "Get it on ice fast. The fish will sell themselves."

The fish hold was amidships, behind a tiny storage locker where I occasionally slept. It was divided into wooden pens bedded with a layer of ice. The fish was culled into separate pens by type—haddock, cod, whiting, pollack and dabs—whatever we caught that day. All except the dabs had to be gutted. At first, the smell of the fish, the gas fumes and the stale bilgewater in combination would make me sick. After a while, I got used to it.

We sold our fish to Jewish and Italian merchants on the Old Wharf section of Packard Pier. The price of fish changed by the hour. We rushed to the pier as soon as we had a decent-sized catch because the price fell later in the day.

We moved our catch from boat to wharf in small wicker baskets. At low tide the boat was much lower than the wharf and required a lot of work pulling on ropes attached to the baskets.

This was my earliest training as a fisherman. The work was hard. My father was a good teacher and his advice stayed with me. I would later teach my four sons to fish as my father taught me.

My brother Vincent's birth in 1924 was difficult. I often heard my mother tell her women friends that Vincent (or Jimmy, as we called him) was a breech birth. The midwife who attended didn't know how to handle a breech. She pulled and helped the wrong way. Jimmy was hurt. By the time the doctor arrived, the damage was done. Jimmy was partially paralyzed and slightly retarded.

At first, my mother didn't know these things of her son. Jimmy was a beautiful baby, a chubby blond. My mother began to notice he was slow to grab at things. She tried to get medical help for him when he couldn't walk. She always tried to get help for Jimmy. When the doctors told her the truth, she refused to believe them.

Because we were so poor, Jimmy was taken as a ward of the state. My mother took me as translator when she visited Jimmy at the clinics and hospitals. When Jimmy was home, the state allotted him three gallons of milk and some eggs and butter. It was my job to go to the agency in Haymarket Square to pick up the food. My mother gave all of us children a small portion.

The state sent Jimmy to the Boston Floating Hospital one summer.

The ship was tied up at North End Park Pier. My mother was busy with six other children. Often she had me go with Jimmy on his regular visits to the hospital. I remember feeling the ocean breeze on hot summer days as the Floating Hospital cruised up and down the harbor.

I learned to wash, diaper and feed Jimmy and became friendly with some of the staff. One of the nurses told me I handled babies as well as she did. The truth is that I loved those trips; there was so much milk and good food for me to eat.

My mother deeply touched me with her devotion to Jimmy. God bless her soul! It seemed all the world was against her sometimes as she tried to raise seven children. Jimmy never left my parents' home. When she died in 1945, my mother had instilled a similar devotion to Jimmy in all her children. "See that Jimmy gets a break in life," she had said. Jimmy continued to live with my father for more than twenty years after my mother's death. My sister Rosalie and her husband, Tony DaCruz, made Jimmy a member of their family when my father died. He still lives with Rosalie and Tony today.

The year of Vincent's birth, my sister Pauline married Lawrence Scola and moved from Boston to Gloucester. She was only sixteen when she got married, yet she was like a second mother to the rest of us children. Her marriage brought my father a partner on his boat. Lawrence treated all of us like brothers. We all loved him. He and I were crewmates on half a dozen boats during the next twenty-five years.

My mother missed Pauline after she moved. She and I took the Boston and Maine train out to Cape Ann almost every week. I fell in love with Gloucester instantly. There were tree-lined streets leading to a busy waterfront and clean harbor. Pretty soon I was making the trip alone. My mother would load me up with packages of homemade food for Pauline.

Pauline and her husband rented a tiny apartment in the eaves of a house on Western Avenue. Across the street was a mile-long promenade along the harbor. In the middle of the walkway was a statue of a fisherman at the wheel. It was the most beautiful harbor I had ever seen. I wanted Gloucester for my hometown.

Pauline invited me to stay in Gloucester during the summer of 1926. I helped with her first son, Joseph. The baby died after a year. I never knew why. I stayed with Pauline to give her company and run errands while Lawrence went on ten-day mackerel trips. Pauline was very depressed at the loss of her child. She urged my mother to visit often, even after my mother became pregnant again. My youngest sister, Rosalie, was born in December of 1927 and one year later Pauline gave birth to my niece, Katie.

My mother and sister insisted on raising Rosalie and Katie together, and between the two of them—and me—we finally convinced my father to move to Gloucester.

Our Commercial Court apartment was high above the harbor in a neighborhood called the Fort. We had four rooms for eight people. Everyone was happy to be in Gloucester. The Fort teemed with life. Almost everyone was Italian, and lived here because of fishing. The Fort had been just that, a fort in the Revolution, then a home for the waves of immigrants needed to work the fishing boats.

We rented from the Lupo family. We had electricity and an inside toilet for the first time in our lives, but still no bathtub. My mother dragged a great big tub for washing clothes into the kitchen to scrub us clean.

An Irish family, the Norrises, lived below us. On the back side of the building were the Giammanco, Ciaramitaro and Scola families. Peter Scola and I grew up together. He later became the captain of the *Rose Marie*, and many years later his only daughter, Joanne, married my son Salvatore. A couple of doors down the street was the Randazza family. I would marry their niece, Nina. We all got along nicely in the neighborhood, but when my father thought the twenty dollars for a month's rent was too high, we moved to a fifteen-dollar-a-month flat only a hundred yards away on Beach Court.

During the summers, all the neighborhood kids swam at Pavilion Beach, which was in our backyards. I became pals with Salvatore Brancaleone, whom we called "Bob Custer" after the silent movie cowboy star. Bob and I sometimes earned a little money by gathering up and selling the crazy whiting and herring that beached themselves on Pavilion Beach and were left flapping on the sand as the tide went out. Gloucester was a great place to grow up.

I soon grew from a pale, thin kid to a strong young man. A doctor came to our apartment to examine Jimmy about a month after we arrived in our new home. My mother had the doctor look at me. He then diagnosed that I had malnutrition. He told my mother to feed me half-cooked red meat and plenty of milk and vegetables.

There were no supermarkets in Gloucester, nor was there an open market like those in the North End. Instead, we bought our food from the backs of trucks that came into the Fort.

Anthony Kyrouz was known as "*San Antonio*" because he gave the Fort families credit on his meat and produce. San Antonio was a Lebanese immigrant. His sons, Joe and Freddy, came in the truck with him. Freddy also later worked at the shoeshine parlor on Main Street. He's been a city clerk now for decades.

Another Lebanese family, the Lattofs of nearby Rockport, ran a farm and sold what they had from a truck every fall. Maria Lattof and her son, Mitch, always came together in a beat-up pickup truck. The Italian families dubbed her *Maria Arabiana.*

Mr. Balzarini was also a regular in the Fort. He sold beef, hot dogs and bologna. His daughter, Rose, drove his truck and made early morning milk deliveries in the neighborhood.

My mother bought the very best she could afford for me after the doctor's visit. Often she haggled with the truck-stand owners. I felt guilty when my younger brothers and sister watched my mother give me the biggest portions. She must have sensed I was getting big enough to earn a man's wage. At least my bad dreams went away.

After we first arrived in Gloucester, Pauline took me in hand and walked me to St. Ann's School. It was the biggest Catholic parish in town. They had a big stone church, with a towering spire, an elementary school, a high school and a small building for the nuns. All of the Italians went to St. Ann's.

St. Ann's School was growing rapidly. They kept the tuition cost down. Even a poor family could scrape together the fees. The nuns told Pauline and me there was no space for one more boy in the middle of the school year. We left disappointed.

I went to the public Hovey School on Washington Street. It was a three-story brick building on a worn-out patch of grass. The work was very difficult for me. Everything was said in English. Nothing reminded me of the Catholic schools in Boston. I fell behind in English and math. Today, I still have trouble pronouncing some English words; Sicilian Italian is my first instinct. It wasn't long before I could do scratch-pad math as fast as any dealer on the water-front, though. I didn't want anyone taking advantage of me by moving the decimal point.

My mother got me into St. Ann's. I got jumped on my first day of school there. The nuns had introduced me as "Rosario," my birth-certificate name, and the kids at lunch taunted me as "Rosie" and the "Boston boy." They insulted me and I had two fights in the schoolyard. The real showdown came the next day. I was walking on Middle Street near the old YMCA when five kids came over a wall and surrounded me. I tried to defend myself against their punches, but there were too many for me. A bystander jumped in on my side. We held them off and walked away together. My new friend was Salvatore Ciaramitaro. We became best buddies. I stayed in school only two more years and Salvatore was almost always at my side. We fished together on a few boats and became *compari.* He became a very successful businessman with his brother, Peter, and as owners of Gloucester Grocery and Boat Supply, outfitted hundreds of boats over the years.

The way Fate works. Of the five who jumped me, all became

good friends. All were from the same neighborhood. All were from the same background. Salvatore Curcuru and I are *compari*. I was best man at his wedding, he at mine. He's godfather to my oldest, I to his. His brother, Nicky, was also in the gang. He's been a full-time fisherman all his life. John B. Aiello captained boats, including the *Sacred Heart* and the *Cape Cod*. He's retired. His brother, Anthony, is still fishing. There was one girl in the gang: Salvatore Curcuru's aunt, Mary Parisi. Salvatore Nicastro and I were crewmates on the *Bethulia* when he got engaged to Mary Parisi. I was an usher at their wedding and reminded Mary of our fight on Middle Street. Salvatore Nicastro became a top-notch captain and boat owner. He founded Felicia Oil Company, one of the waterfront's biggest wharves and supply depots.

I was now a big, strong kid. I was anxious to make some friends, so I defended the little kids against bullies in the schoolyard. One of them I helped, Stanley Boudreau, grew up to be mayor. Another, Ralph Greely, became a Marine. We became good friends. He came to my family's house to say good-bye to my mother and me when he enlisted. That was the last time I saw him. He died a young man in the battle at Iwo Jima, another who was too young to die.

Teddy Williams, his brother, Big Bill Williams, Tucky Holmes and Roy Goulart played rough-and-tumble football on what little grass we had in the schoolyard. Williams later gained fame as a Gloucester High and Boston College halfback. Holmes and Goulart played high school ball on winning teams.

There were scores of Fort kids. Charlie Curcuru and his brothers: Gene, Sam (Red Top), Philip and Joe. Their family owned Producers Fish Company and lived next to us at 19 Commercial Street. Salvatore Aiello ("Sanapolly") and his brother Paul; Albert Genovese, whose father fished with my father; Tommy Molino and Tommy Randazza (Jack Brady). Tommy Randazza later became my brother-in-law. Johnny Keresey and Joe Rubino and his cousins: Larry and Joe ("Compare Pepe") Parisi. Sammy Frontiero, who later captained the *Lady in Blue*; the Pascucci boys; Donny Ciaramitaro and his brothers, Danny, Sam, Donny, Joe (J.J.), and Fat Pauley, who later became my brother-in-law; and Mike Frontiero. Albert Catania, Busty Palazzola and his brother Tony, whom we called "Tony Carnera" after the heavyweight fighter Primo Carnera.

There were Tommy Frontiero ("Ticcatanna") and his brother Paul, Vito Misuaca and his brother Natale; Nofie Demetri and his brother Gus; Jimmy Bertolino ("Spaba") and his brothers. The Bertolino family owned an Italian bakery and grocery store. Joe Grillo, who later became mayor, and his brother, Charlie; Larry and Nick Nicolosi, whose father owned a fruit and vegetable store on the corner of

Pascucci Wharf and Commercial Street; Frank Palmisano and his brother, Charlie; Tommy Favazza and his brother, Patsy. The Favazzas' father started the St. Peter Fiesta by donating the St. Peter statue.

Also, there were Tommy Lupo, Salvatore Brancaleone and Frankie Favazza, whose father, Petro, supplied fishermen and boats with gear and groceries; Leo Mione and his brothers, Peter and Johnny. The Mione brothers all became fishing captains. John Randazza ("Pee Wee") and his brothers; Tootsie Parisi and his brothers; Rosario Giammanco ("Sasor") and his brother, Iggy; Charley Orlando and his brothers; Salvatore and Peter Ciaramitaro; Tom Parisi and his brother, Fat Parisi; Sammy Frontiero ("Cigar Butts") and his brothers Benny ("Monte Carlo"), Peter ("Petizzy"); Larry, Gaspar and Sofie Palazzola; Donny Favazza, whom we called "Morton Downey" after the popular singer; and the Parisi boys, Nack, Fat Tink, Sam, Charley, Mike and Joe; and Michael Frontiero ("Crabs").

I had some special friends: "Speed" Lucido, "Busty" Scola ("Small Ears") and his brother Spikey; and Joe, Nick, Scrody and Sammy Novello. Tommy Lupo, James "Spaba" Bertolino, Sammy Curcuru, Sammy Ciaramitaro and Joe "Saginaw" Loiacano later became my *compari*.

The Sicilian families in the Fort were the Nicastros, Randazzas, Ciolinos, Tarantinos, Ciluffos, Ventimiglias, Agrussos, Scolas, Lavascos, Sinagras, Loiacanos, Linquatas and Palazzolas. There were two or three ways to spell some of the names. The ambition of all the boys was to become fishermen and maybe captains. Many succeeded; some lost their lives trying.

While I was still in St. Ann's school, I often spent my lunch periods reeling nets on the waterfront and my afternoons delivering the *Gloucester Daily Times* to make money. I even sold fish door-to-door for a time.

Gill netting boats used huge nets to trap fish. The nets were arranged to catch whole schools of fish as the gills got caught in the mesh of the nets. When the boats came in, the nets had to be dried and unsnarled on the docks. Kids got paid twenty-five cents for each box, which contained nine hundred feet of net. I could put up two boxes during lunch. The City Hall bells would ring when I had fifteen minutes to get back to school. Sometimes I was late. Once I started a box, I had to finish it or else I wouldn't get paid. The nuns kept me after school for being late, but I would sneak out and deliver my papers. The next day I had to explain again that I couldn't stay after school because I'd lose customers on my route. The nuns didn't understand and there was much tension between us. The Sisters of Mercy could be very harsh on a youngster. Reeling nets and selling newspapers made me six or seven dollars a week! I gave it all to my mother.

When a navy ship came into port, I had another way to make money. An old woman on Western Avenue sold homemade wine to the Italians in the neighborhood. It was good, strong stuff and the sailors loved it. Wine was no big deal to me. I had grown up with it, so no one blinked an eye when I would buy a couple of jugs from the old woman. Sometimes I even got credit. Instead of taking it home to my parents, I hustled the wine to shore leave sailors at the town landing with a thirst for a wild time. A four-dollar gallon netted me one dollar. I always found ways to make a buck. It was Prohibition and I was twelve.

A FULL SHARE

Shortly after my family arrived in Gloucester, my father and Lawrence, who were now fishing partners, decided that the old *703E* was too unsteady in heavy weather and too slow to get back and forth from the best fishing grounds offshore. The new partners scratched together $2,000 for part payment on a new boat. It was an ambitious venture.

The boat was built in Ipswich. It had two-inch planks the entire length of her fifty-two feet and a larger, deeper fo'c'sle and 30,000 pounds more capacity in the fish hold than the *703E*. She stood two feet higher out of the water than the *703E* and had the sleek lines of a Coast Guard boat. She was twelve tons and powered by a 45 hp Bridgeport engine with a manual clutch and automatic oil pumping. She was about twice as fast as the *703E*. She was proudly named for my sister Pauline. As I recognized later, she was a boat far ahead of her time.

A local bank financed $3,000 towards the purchase. Where the family's $2,000 came from, I never knew. A fish processing company on the waterfront backed up the bank's notes. My father and Lawrence were obligated to sell their catches to that processor, no matter what the prices. The processor kept the upper hand that way. At the time, I'm sure it looked like a fair and square deal to my family. As they later learned, this particular processor was no friend.

The *Pauline S.* was launched at Ipswich in 1928. I was eleven years old and very excited. On our maiden voyage, however, the main bearing burned out and the Coast Guard towed us in. Unknown to us, some broken glass had gotten into the oil during the engine installation and choked off the oil line.

My father screamed bloody murder at the boatyard. A glass casing was smashed during installation and nobody had bothered to change the pump line. Now glass was in the entire engine! The boatyard people guaranteed the first repair job, but it wasn't enough. Months later we were still having engine troubles and the warranty had long since expired.

Repairs kept the *Pauline S.* from fishing. The bank notes kept coming due. Nineteen twenty-nine was a rough year. Hard times were upon the fishing industry. Even the processors were hurting, though it was sometimes hard to feel sorry for them. Haddock dropped to two cents a pound. Cod fell to a penny a pound and hake sold for sixty cents per hundred pounds at Gorton-Pew Fisheries, one of the few places that would even buy it.

Under these circumstances, my father and Lawrence jumped at a one-time opportunity to do something different. The lighthouse keeper at Matinicus Rock in Maine was being transferred to Thatcher's Island in Rockport. He needed his furniture moved. The keeper offered $150 for the job.

On the trip to Matinicus, we started out in strong southwest tail winds. As we approached the light, the weather worsened and sent us into Matinicus Island Harbor, across a narrow channel from the light. After two days, the winds stopped. We stood a hundred yards off the light as a couple of dories ferried furniture to us. It was packed in the fish hold. This was a sad statement on how poorly we were filling the hold with fish.

Our cargo included five crates of live chickens. We also got talked into towing a small lobster boat back to Thatcher's Island, even though it wasn't in the original agreement with the lightkeeper.

Our bad luck was at least consistent, as winds turned around from the southwest as we turned for home. Three times we had to stop to pump the lobster boat dry and save it from sinking. The poor chickens got seasick and looked dead. Seventeen hours of headwinds later, we anchored off Thatcher's Island and waited for the lightkeeper to send a dory for his furniture. I checked the chicken crates and found three dozen eggs to take home to my mother. Those crazy birds had started laying eggs as soon as the boat steadied at anchor.

Lawrence and I were invited in for breakfast when we went to the North Light to collect our cash pay. I explained how rough it was coming across the Gulf of Maine as the lightkeeper's wife prepared eggs and ham and coffee. As I talked, the lightkeeper agreed to pay us an extra fifty, for saving the lobster boat.

My father was very happy when he found out we got $200. I was a very tired twelve-year-old and happily fell asleep in the fo'c'sle. There was only one two-hundred-dollar furniture trip aboard the *Pauline S.* The final blow to my father came after he decided to sell his catches to Boston fish processors. He told me that some Gloucester dealers had made a habit of clipping fishermen on the net weight of a catch. The local dealers also paid a penny or two less per pound than the Boston dealers. The two cents supposedly covered the cost of trucking the fish back to Boston. My father said baloney and he split his trips between Gloucester and Boston.

My father and Lawrence fell behind on their bank payments. The local processor who had vouched for the loan dishonored the notes to spite my father. The bank promptly foreclosed and attached a lien on the boat. All of this was done without my father knowing it. My father went down to the boat one morning and found a sheriff standing on the wharf. The sheriff said the *Pauline S.* had been seized and blocked my father's path to the deck. My father went berserk. He and Lawrence and the crew had spent much of the night before baiting all twenty tubs of trawls. Now more money and time was being wasted. The law was cruel and he couldn't read the sheriff's papers. My father spoke no English; the sheriff spoke no Sicilian. My father pulled a knife and chased the sheriff from the wharf. Later, more deputies came and took the boat away.

My father was arrested, but he never had to go to court. Still, his spirit was broken. He had no heart for living anymore. All his money was lost. He must have known he would never own another boat and his ambitions were dashed. My poor mother bore the brunt of my father's financial problems. He blamed the whole world for being against him. We all listened, but only my mother heard him. She cried often, but tried to keep it to herself.

The fall of that year was really rough. My father wasn't working. The family was broke. Thanksgiving Day was coming up and we had no food. I found myself resorting to old habits of wandering the streets. I was twelve years old now and no longer worried my mother that I'd come home slung over the shoulders of a policeman or lifeguard. Now I was worried about her as I walked out of the Fort, thinking about how sad she looked on the day before Thanksgiving.

I found a crowd standing in front of the fire station on School Street. Some people were waiting in lines and others were coming out of the building carrying boxes. I went in and got a big box of repaired toys and secondhand books for my four little brothers and sister. I met a friend as I walked home with the toys. He said the Salvation Army on Pleasant Street was giving away baskets of food.

I stashed the box of toys at home and ran to the Salvation Army. They were visible in Gloucester year-round; often their small band played music on the corner of Main and Duncan streets. Since they were Protestants or *Protestantes*, it was a sacrilege to listen. It was even worse to believe.

After a short wait in line, there was a brief interview just inside the door of the place. Nobody asked about religion. I told them we were poor and had no food for Thanksgiving. I said the boats were all in and not even fish was available for the holiday. They gave me a basket with a turkey, vegetables, sweet potatoes, a pumpkin, apples, nuts and cranberries. I had never seen a cranberry. As I walked home with my basket, I tasted it, thinking it was a cherry. It was very sour, but I wouldn't spit it out.

Upon my arrival home, my mother took one look at me and the basket and accused me, "Where did you steal it?" "The good people at the Salvation Army are giving food away to the needy and we are the needy," I said. My mother praised God and thanked me. The feast of Thanksgiving was memorable. Even today I clean my pockets of silver whenever I see the Salvation Army donation kettle.

We shared our good times and hard times in the one-big-family atmosphere of the Fort. There were so many people living in our tenement building that someone was always standing in a doorway or leaning out a window. All the families mixed freely for hours of story-swapping and card-playing. When we kids were lucky enough to have a couple of coins, we could run off to the movies.

One night when I was almost thirteen, all the families were trading stories in the home of Cosmo Filetto, Sr., when I was offered a job "site" on the eighty-six-foot seiner *St. Theresa*. I was delighted. The *St. Theresa* was captained by the very able Philip Filetto, Cosmo's son. The boat was owned by the Filetto family and Cosmo's brother-in-law, Fat Parisi.

I was assigned as cabin boy to the cook, Cosmo Filetto, Sr. No one ever got rich as a cabin boy, but most fishermen were cabin boys first. I washed dishes, ran errands, and helped out on deck when the fish came over the side. I was paid the odd change left over when the fifteen-man crew shared a trip's profits. On a good trip, I made twelve dollars.

At last I was out from under the watchful and critical eyes of my father and among grown men from the Fort. I was determined to fit in among these hard men and learn everything about this trade called "purse seining."

Seining required a much bigger boat and more men than hook-and-line tub trawling. In fact, seining required a couple of boats. The objective was to trap whole schools of mackerel or herring. A 40-foot open seine boat and a 14-foot dory were used to draw a net around the fish. The seines were 220 fathoms long and 20 fathoms deep.

Corks and lead weights kept the net spread from the ocean's surface and weighted the bottom.

The seine net was set out in a large circle. At the beginning of the net was the "keg," which was attached to the dory. The seine boat crew would pay out the net and "lead line," complete the circle and come back to the dory. Then, in a big hurry, both the keg and lead lines would be drawn tight or pursed by a donkey engine attached to the seine boat. It got its name because it was stubborn and sometimes wouldn't start. This would seal off the bottom of the net so the fish couldn't dive and escape. Then, using only our backs and arms, the whole crew would draw the net closer to the keg and the dory. The net twine closest to the keg was thick and called the "bunt"; that farthest from from the keg was thinner. When the bunt was a tight ball of fish, the mother boat came alongside the seine boat and used a dip net to scoop the fish out of the bunt and bail them on board for storage below deck.

By the time I was fourteen, I had moved up from cabin boy to doryman on the *St. Theresa* and eventually was paid half a share. My job was to handle the keg line while my partner rowed the dory. I was picked for this job because I was the lightest and nimblest crew member.

I spent two summers seining aboard the *St. Theresa*. In the meantime, I started working tub trawling trips aboard the Parco boats, the *Maria Concetta* and the *Marianna*. It was aboard the *Maria Concetta* that I learned the perils of the ocean and aboard the *Marianna* that I earned my first full share.

We were on a fairly routine trip with Cosmo Parco as captain and a crew made up of my father; Parco's father-in-law, Pepe Orlando; his cousin, Nino Orlando; and Frank Sinagra, who was a barber by trade but sometimes went out fishing out of boredom. "The kid works twice as hard as the rest of us," said Sinagra, talking about me. "Give him a full share. He only gets half because he's a kid."

I was happy to hear these words. My father stood by waiting for the captain's reaction. It wasn't proper for a father to speak up for his son. Crews didn't give up any part of a share easily. Half a share more for me meant less for them. Captain Cosmo nodded his head, and yes, I had my full share.

In all my years of fishing I never believed in hard-and-fast traditions or superstitions aboard the boat. Many of the old-timers would give you hell for putting a hatch cover down the wrong way or allowing a woman on deck. I fished with some guys who swore that tobacco left near the compass would cause it to get drunk. Red-ribboned bull's horns kept away the evil spirits. There was no question in my mind that fishermen needed the benefit of luck, but I believed you make your own through hard work and determination, not by keeping women off the boats.

The *Maria Concetta* and the *Marianna* were driven hard by the Parco brothers. We were among the first tub trawlers in the Italian fleet to steam into the offshore grounds of Platt's Bank and Phippeny Ledge, more than seventy miles from Gloucester Harbor. We often came home with fish hold full of cod and a mix of haddock, hake and cusk. Sometimes we caught as much as 2,500 pounds of halibut, which paid top dollar. These grounds were virgin, untouched by the wide-sweeping draggers that would come later.

The Parco family owned the boats without substantial debt and sold their catches in Boston for a higher price. From Gloucester to the fishing grounds to Boston was more than two hundred miles round trip. Fuel tanks were very close to empty when we tied up in Boston. Captain Salvatore saved us a lot of aggravation one afternoon when he ordered the *Maria Concetta* to anchor and "lay to" in a gale. The gale was blowing northwest into the bow as we struggled to get into Boston. We would have run out of fuel fighting those winds if Captain Salvatore hadn't dropped anchor and waited two days for a change in the weather. As it was, we chugged into the harbor on what must have been fumes.

A typical trip aboard the *Maria Concetta* began at midnight, when we shoved off from Matt Frontiero's wharf and set a course for the Provincetown Light. By dawn, we'd have live bait, usually herring, from the trap boats outside Provincetown. We baited lines while steaming to the fishing grounds. At first I felt a little uneasy about being seventy miles from the nearest land. I threw myself into the work at hand and put the dangers out of my mind.

It usually took two or three days to make our trip and return with a full fish hold. After we landed in Boston, there was more work. We had already baited, set, and hauled the trawls; culled, cut, gutted and washed the catch; but now we had to unload and sell the fish. We didn't want to pay the extra money to have lumpers move our catches to the docks. We did it ourselves.

The fish was dumped into 500-pound boxes and loaded on the back of pushcarts. This was hard enough at high tide but even worse at low. Our boats had no masts and all the fish had to be hoisted in baskets on ropes by hand to the dock. There was plenty of use for a pitchfork on the wharf. The dealers gave us receipts for the net weight.

With the fish sold, the trawl lines had to be overhauled and twenty tubs put up for the next day. While the other crew tended the tubs, my job as the youngest was to wash out the pens in the fish hold and wash down the deck. I drew all the water from over the side in buckets. The fo'c'sle where we slept and cooked meals on a cast-iron Shipmate stove was scrubbed down to the floorboards.

Finally, we shared up: the cost of fuel, ice and food came off the top of gross receipts. The net receipts were divided into equal shares, one for each crew member, the captain, and the boat itself. Usually, the captain was the owner and he got two shares. If the captain didn't own the boat, he got one share plus a "per," a percentage of the owner's share, usually 15 or 20 percent. A good four-day trip could bring fifty dollars a man. That was pretty good money in those days.

More often we shared up a lot less than fifty dollars each. The Depression worsened and the number of trips we made fell off. Banks failed, credit disappeared, work at processing and boat repair shops fell to a halt. Across the country people felt on the brink of total disaster. Millions had no work; millions more had plenty of misery.

President Roosevelt came in with a lot of new government agencies and tried to put the country right. His programs never touched the fishermen. I guess we were too small a minority compared to the farmers or steel workers.

LIFE ON THE *SALVATORE*

In the spring of 1932 I got a site aboard the mackerel seiner *Salvatore*. We rigged up for a two-month trip to fishing grounds off Cape May, New Jersey. Vito Locrico was captain and we were a fifteen-man crew.

Cape May was port of call for boats from North Carolina to Maine when mackerel was hitting the offshore waters. Gloucester had more than its share of boats in the seasonal mackerel trade. A smart and ambitious captain and an able crew could make money on mackerel. Fulton Market, at the tip of Manhattan Island, was the jackpot. Freight trains left Cape May regularly, but fishermen nearly broke their necks to get the first catch going to New York.

I was very eager to go on my first long trip away from home. I had been on ten-day trips at sea, but usually with crews that included my father. I had my full share, a good reputation for being a hard worker and I was growing bigger and stronger every day. The crew of the *Salvatore* arrived on the wharf about midnight on March 19, the feast of St. Joseph, one of the special religious celebrations for fishermen. Men carried small cardboard cases and bags, full of clothes for the trip. Nobody watched us off as we left Gloucester.

The lockers below deck were stocked with all kinds of foods, the fish hold with twenty tons of crushed ice, fuel tanks at capacity. The run to Cape May took less than three days in good weather but much longer if the weather turned bad and forced us into either Block Island or New York City.

The crew was made up of a good many young men: Carlo Ciaramitaro, Billy Ragusa, Busty Ciolino, Frank Lucido, Phil Cusumano, Frank Militello, and Peter Conti, Sr. All later became captains and boat owners. My sister's husband, Lawrence, was helmsman. During the next fifty years, Busty Ciolino and Peter Conti would save my life; I'd be the best man at Frank Militello's wedding and Frank Lucido's granddaughter would marry my son.

As the *Salvatore* steamed past the breakwater and into open sea, I stood on deck and watched the familiar silhouette of church spires and City Hall disappear behind me. The sky was light with stars and more than half the moon. The ocean glittered. In the pilothouse, Captain Locrico stood at the wheel under a tiny light. His eyes glanced at the charts, the compass and our course. Once beyond the Eastern Point buoy, the first watch took control of the boat. The crew was paired off, and one man would hold the wheel and one man would watch from the bow. Each watch lasted two hours. It was my first trip south and a new adventure; I could not sleep. I kept the forward watch company. I wanted to see everything and especially Cape Cod Canal. The rest of the crew was sleeping down below.

At dawn I took the wheel. Once, I called the captain to deck to point out a passenger steamer off bow. Captain Locrico did not grumble when awakened. Few good captains did.

The *Salvatore* had fair luck on my first trip to Cape May. We always fished at night, when we could find the mackerel better. Captain Locrico would climb to the crosstrees in our rigging and spot the fish for us. Mackerel travel in schools on the surface and when excited at night they leave a very visible wake. Fishermen called it "fire in the water." Later, I learned it was the phosphorus in the ocean being churned up as the fish swam.

On our first trip out of Cape May, we caught 30,000 pounds of mackerel and rushed into port, hoping to be the first boat to arrive. We got first prize, twenty-five cents a pound, and were off to a fabulous start. Prices could change like the wind, and fell off sharply later in the spring. Coming in on the last day of April, for example, the *Salvatore* was loaded with 65,000 pounds. There were no other boats in Cape May when we landed. The whole crew thought it was going to be a big payday. The dealers refused our fish. Unknown to us, most of the other boats in the fleet had landed at Fulton Market in New York earlier that day and the price there was one and one-half cents a pound. Our Cape May dealer knew this but said nothing. This was long before the days of telephone and radio communications between boats. We had two choices, neither of them good. We could either dump our fish back at sea or take a chance and ship the fish by train freight to New York and take the market price, whatever that might be, when our fish arrived. We took the chance.

Three weeks later, back in Gloucester, our check was waiting. A whole sixty cents. The dealers had taken out for ice, barrels, freight and labor on the wharf. Our net pay was less than a penny per thousand pounds of fish! That check was never cashed. It was framed and hung on the wall of Peter Favazza's grocery and ship's chandlery store in the Fort. Fishing is a crazy business and that check was the perfect symbol.

A sense of humor aboard the boats was the best cure for both payday disappointment and boredom. There were no radios, records, or television. During the hot, calm days of summer, tired of card games and waiting for fish, the crew wanted to jump over the railing for a swim. Frequent enough sightings of shark fins made this a bad idea.

Sometimes, a spontaneous water fight would break out and everyone would act like children. Even Captain Locrico and cook Sam Trupiano were fair game in the fights. I recall lead linesman Tom Foley starting things off one afternoon and fleeing to the fo'c'sle. He left us dripping wet as he pulled the hatch cover closed. Someone found a can of hot ground peppers in the pilothouse; this would flush Foley out of the fo'c'sle. The peppers went down the smokestack and into the stove. Foley burst on deck gasping for air. Everyone had a bucket of water ready for him. Foley took it in grand style, holding his Irish temper while one bucket after the other was emptied on him.

Captain Locrico, meanwhile, had climbed to the crosstrees forty feet above the deck. He looked pretty safe up there. He wasn't safe. We formed a vertical bucket brigade all the way up the rigging and cooled him off, too.

Mackerel fishing was fiercely competitive, each boat always looking out for itself and each crew showing off with such things as how fast it could pull its seine lines in. Often several boats would be laying to near each other to spot fish. Occasionally, when the captain of one boat sighted commotion on the deck of another, he assumed mackerel had been sighted and steered a quick course for that boat, hoping to catch some himself. Realizing the reason for all the fuss, the captain and crew would sometimes join the water fight, and pretty soon more than one boat would be involved.

At night there was storytelling. Some stories had been told to fishermen for generations; others were modern tales. Some men became very practiced in this art. Aboard the *Salvatore*, Paul Russo told the Sicilian version of the Holy Crusades of the Middle Ages. We huddled in our bunks as we listened while he read from his book. It was animated entertainment, complete with sword thrusts. Russo was an older, well-educated man with family still in Sicily. In later years, when radio and television came aboard the boats, many of the traditional stories were lost to the ages.

For an inquisitive youngster, the endless hours of waiting for fish could be spent learning something new on deck. Tom Foley took an interest in me and devoted hours to showing me how to splice rope, tie knots and mend nets. With a twinkle in his eyes, he once told me, "I have a nice girl for you someday." I was almost sixteen years old and just starting to notice girls. Tom's daughter died a couple years later and Tom was a sad man after that. He was very religious, and more than once I caught him on the stern saying his rosary. His son, Bob, became a fisherman and, now retired, serves on the Gloucester Housing Authority.

Felix Hogan, or "Captain" Hogan, was the only other non-Sicilian on the *Salvatore*. He was sixty-five years old and supposedly retired but he worked the deck with the rest of us. He loved his wine and would dance a jig and excite me with his tales of chasing girls in every port. He was a Newfoundlander or Nova Scotian and a former captain, according to him. He carried his sextant with him on every trip. More than once, he tried to explain the workings of the instrument to Captain Vito but his lessons were lost on the captain because he couldn't figure out the degrees and numbers. Captain Locrico preferred his "dead reckoning" to all other methods. He was damn good at it, and lucky.

Whenever the *Salvatore* went into new ports, I went forward to the bow and paid attention to the boat's maneuverings between the various buoys. I'd pick out certain landmarks and make mental notes for later reference. Captain Locrico noticed my interest and showed me how to use the charts and parallel ruler to set a course. This is how I learned enough to navigate and captain my own boat later on. I had no formal education, but hands-on experience never failed me.

It was never all work on the mackerel trips. Sometimes we got time ashore. In New Bedford one afternoon, after landing a trip, two pals and I washed, dressed up in our best clean clothes and walked to the Olympic Theater for a picture show. We went to the diner next door for a cup of coffee afterwards. The owner had shortcakes, topped with whipped cream and strawberries, lined up along the counter. I ordered one and quickly downed it. I had another, and another. This kind of food was never served aboard the boats and I was determined to have my fill.

"You must really love to eat strawberry shortcake," said the owner as he watched the third one disappear.

"I love strawberry shortcake," I replied. "I could eat every one you've got in this diner."

"I bet you can't," he said.

"I'll tell you what," I said. "You put the shortcakes in front of me and I'll start eating. If I can't eat all of them, then I'll pay you for what I ate. If I eat all of them, then I don't have to pay a dime."

"Okay. Let's see you do it," he said.

All the customers looked on with great amusement as I polished off five, ten, fifteen shortcakes, pausing occasionally for a cold glass of milk. Twenty-three shortcakes later, I dropped my fork on the empty plate. Not a single piece of the delicious stuff was left in the diner.

The customers were all having a good laugh at the diner owner. He pointed at me, narrowed his eyes and asked my name.

"I'm Salve Testaverde from Gloucester," I answered.

"Well, Salve Testaverde of Gloucester, you get out of here right now and never set foot in this diner again!"

THE *VICTORIA*

By October, the seine boats were high and dry on the scores of wooden wharves shooting into the harbor from every cove. We'd strip the nets of the corks and lead lines and stow the gear away at the end of every season. Otherwise, the nets and ropes would rot and have to be replaced in the spring. Of course, we had no nylon then.

Dragging was still a mystery to me. The *Salvatore* was off Norfolk, Virginia, and I was standing on the wharf. Only six skilled fishermen, including my brother-in-law, manned the *Salvatore*, making for a lucrative trade. Seining required many more hands, and shares.

I returned to tub trawling and hook-and-line, this time aboard the *Victoria*, a 42-foot "guinea" trawler, captained by Vito Favalora. His son, Sofie, was my age. Besides Sofie and myself, the crew was Favalora's son-in-law, Lawrence, Gaspar Palazzola, and Big John, who were both in their thirties. We got along fine, always speaking English, in contrast to the other boats, where the majority spoke Italian. Most of us spoke both. We were the way all boats should be, hardworking and happy. We were a contented lot of youngsters.

We'd set two strings of trawl lines within a quarter mile of each other, eight tubs. In the fine weather, we used one dory to haul half the lines. In fog or even hazy weather, dories were too dangerous. We were afraid of sudden storms or parting a trawl line. You don't want to be cut off from the mother boat when visibility disappears. If that happens, you're lost. You're at the mercy of nature. This dilemma put a terrific load on the captain. He had to make the right decision on whether or not to put the dory out with two men in it. With the dory, the work load was cut in half. The boat would haul eight tubs and the dory would haul the other eight. That could end the workday very early in the afternoon.

Larry and I handled the dory when the weather was fair. We got along nicely, although seven years apart in age. I'd do the hauling because I hated to cut and gut fish. I had done enough heading and gutting aboard the *Maria Concetta* and the *Marianna* to last a lifetime. We'd haul four tubs early in the morning, then have the boat come alongside so Larry could pitch as much as two thousand pounds of fish, mostly cod, on the deck of the *Victoria*. The crew would give us four empty tubs to haul back again.

At the break, I'd often go aboard the boat and pretend I needed a drink of water. Once the Captain shouted at me, "Salve, you already have a gallon of water in the dory. Why do you come aboard for a drink?" I'd remind him we might need the water in the dory in the event of an emergency. The skipper realized my purpose in going aboard. Most mornings, before going out for the day, we'd buy two dozen jelly doughnuts from Mr. Feldman, who ran a Jewish bakery on Commercial Street. Every time we went out in the dory the other crewmen would eat the doughnuts, leaving nothing for Larry and me. I'd hide an extra dozen in a paper bag aboard the *Victoria* and retrieve them during the breaks between sets of tubs. As the dory moved away from the *Victoria*, I'd pull the bag from under my shirt and say, "Hey, Larry. Look what I have here." We'd have a good laugh and eat the dozen between us.

I passed fall and winter on the *Victoria*. I'd save two dollars from every trip. The rest went to my parents. I had it in my mind to buy a car. I knew I could get one for $300. I stuffed the one-, five-, and a few ten-dollar bills under the carpet in the bedroom I shared with my four brothers.

The five of us slept in one large bed. Sometimes I got kicked in the face, and how many times did Jimmy wet the bed and I'd wake up in the middle of the night with a wet back? Finally, I squawked to my mother. "I'm too big to sleep with them; I want my own bed." To my surprise, I got a cot and slept in a small corridor between my parents' room and the kitchen. At least I was alone in bed now.

During this time, Lawrence Palazzola, my dory partner, got the bad news. He wasn't feeling well and stayed ashore to visit a doctor. The tests showed spots on his lungs. He needed further treatment. We had gone out without him and set the trawl lines. Captain Vito Favaloro asked if I would go out in the dory alone to haul the lines. I said yes, and I did. I never minded being alone in a dory again.

Late in February, we had a springlike day. The weather was calm and very clear. It fooled the captain. He set the trawl lines in one long string, instead of lining them up parallel. I went into the dory alone and was about five miles from the boat when a thick fog bank engulfed us. I continued to haul toward the *Victoria* as I could hear the pop-pop of her engine muffler. Every time the engine started, it puffed. The engine was a Lothrop with no clutch and had to be started and stopped frequently.

The sound of the muffler gave me a false sense of security. I had finished hauling one tub trawl line when I heard the sound all fishermen dread—the fog horn of a large steamship coming in direct line to the *Victoria* and my dory. I could hear the crew signal the ship their position with a hand-held fog horn. The ship just kept coming closer and closer. The ship's foghorn was now blaring. Finally, it passed the *Victoria*. It was coming for me.

I tied the trawl line to an oarlock and frantically blew my foghorn, to no avail. The steamer was bearing down on me. I could hear the roar and thumping of the steamer's engines as she closed in on me. I wanted to cut the trawl line and row away, but my good sense forced me to stay. If I had cut the line, I'd have been lost to the *Victoria*, which was likely to miss me in the fog.

The ship continued cutting a path toward me. My fog horn was blaring in my trembling hands as I watched the steamer's huge shadow pass over me. My heart was pounding as hard as the pistons in the steamer's engine. I estimated that she was almost 300 feet in length.

Her wake almost swamped me. Many fishermen in dories and boats were run down in this fashion. Usually the ship's skipper and officers never knew they had run down a fisherman. The crew had feared the worst for me. They had witnessed the path the ship had taken. I blew my horn, still shaking. Fifteen minutes later, the *Victoria* answered my calls. The captain had ordered Gaspar Palazzola to cut the trawl lines and put buoys on it. Then he steered a course for me.

Soon the *Victoria* came alongside me, took my fish and trawl line and put the dory aboard in its cradle on deck. I must have looked frightened, for Captain Favaloro handed me a mug of red wine. "I think I'll have one, too," he said.

We hauled the rest of the trawl line from the *Victoria*'s deck and finished later that afternoon. In the early evening, we started the twenty-six-mile steam from Jeffrey's Bank to Cape Ann.

I never told my parents, or later my wife, the things that happened at sea. I told my sons. My philosophy was never tell the womenfolk anything. It only made for unnecessary worrying.

After three weeks Larry was feeling well enough to come out fishing. The doctors told him to take it easy. What else could he do but go fishing? It was his only means of survival and support for his wife and child.

One day we were steaming past Thatcher's Island for the Blue Hills grounds, where the bottom is made up of blue clay banks, when Larry mentioned a rumrunner who had gotten away. Larry said he had heard all kinds of rumors about a Coast Guard cutter chasing the rumrunner the previous night. They had escaped when the boat was lightened considerably by throwing the entire cargo of alcohol over the side.

All that booze was afloat somewhere and the federal boat hadn't stopped to pick it up. The Coast Guard finally gave up its search in the darkness. The word was out on the waterfront.

We reached our spot on the bank to put out our main buoys—we used two red pennants for good visibility—marking the trawl line. We then retraced our course to the first buoy and ran another line along the high spot on the bank. More pennants marked the second line. We had set four tubs when my eyes turned to the northwest. I spied wooden crates floating in the water, some high out of the water, others even with the surface. Half and full cases, we figured. Somebody must have gotten to the half-empty crates and been spooked from taking the whole lot.

We changed our course to northwest and came upon the crates. We checked out the stuff while sounding the bottom to make sure we were still on the bank. The crates contained jugs of 200-proof Belgian and St. Pierre alcohol. There were six gallons to a case. Disregarding all concern for losing the bank, we set our trawl lines in the direction of the other crates. We didn't care about the fish anymore. We wanted the alcohol.

As we came alongside the crates, someone would hold my legs as I dangled over the side, picking up the crates and handing them back to the crew. Everyone was excited now. We collected 29 cases—174 gallons—of 200-proof alcohol. We also found two leaking crates. We salvaged the alcohol in a case of empty milk bottles.

As we came into Gloucester Harbor, we were careful not to expose our spirited catch on deck. We had to pass Ten Pound Island and a 75-foot Coast Guard patrol boat.

Captain Vito Favaloro figured we'd come in at dusk. If the Coast Guard untied their lines and headed for us, we'd meet them halfway, say we had found the alcohol, and claim a ten percent salvage right. Nobody came for us and we tied up at a local wharf as darkness fell.

We split the stuff evenly, half alcohol and half cash. My share was twenty-eight dollars and twenty-four gallons.

We had to give the wharf owner a share because he had seen us unloading the stuff. We wanted to keep his mouth shut. The next day we went out and hauled the trawl lines set the day before. We had a good trip of eight thousand pounds of cod. It was a profitable day, between the contraband and the cod.

My mother and father made whiskey anisetta and rossola, a woman's drink. They cut the alcohol with hot water and sugar flavors; the proof was so high you had to mix it three to one. You could put some on the palm of your hand, light a match, and watch a blue flame erupt—the purity caused to it evaporate quickly without burning your palm. I sold three gallons to my friend Nofrie Demetri when we were crewmates on a seiner. He was getting married and needed the stuff to make whiskey. I got three dollars a gallon and later regretted the sale. You couldn't buy the stuff in those days.

My father saved some until I got married in January, 1940. He still had a quart when my son John was born in November of that year. The alcohol we salvaged in the milk cans was transferred to whiskey bottles and sealed. We kept the bottles stashed on the *Victoria*. Whenever we overhauled our trawl lines in the early morning hours, we'd make hot mugs of coffee spiked with a good shot of 200-proof alcohol. We were the happiest boat in the tub trawling fleet.

Sadly, Larry did not live long after the doctors found spots on his lungs. They were cancerous. Larry was the finest of dorymates. What respect we shared! Our lives depended on one another. Hundreds of hours together in a 14-foot dory made us as close as brothers.

CLOSE CALLS

I returned to the seiner *Salvatore* during the next season for mackerel fishing out of Cape May. We went through the same routines. Frank Lucido would again be my dorymate. He'd man the oars and I'd haul the keg line. By now, all this work had transformed me from a weakling suffering malnutrition to a powerful young man. My waist measurement was thirty-two inches, and my shoulders, forty-eight.

We caught mackerel up and down the coast and landed them at the nearest port, whether it be Cape May, New Jersey; Wildwood, New York; Newport, Rhode Island; New Bedford; Boston; or the northern side of Portland, Maine. I spent four seasons aboard the *Salvatore* and had two close calls on her decks.

It was May of my second season when an attack of appendicitis convinced me I'd die somewhere in Nantucket waters. The day began with the *Salvatore* tied up at Homer's Wharf in New Bedford. We were waiting with the rest of the seining fleet for the southwest winds to die. It was sunny and hot, so some of the fellows and I stripped down and dove off the rigging. The harbor waters were refreshing and we made a good time of it. Meanwhile, the *Salvatore*'s cook, Salvatore Trupiano, was busy preparing a dinner of fresh cauliflower soup-style spaghetti, a pie of fried fresh slices of peppers and eggs, cutlets of fried mackerel and fresh bread.

After all the exercise of swimming, I was hungry and ate with great zeal. I had the appetite of a seventeen-year-old young man with forty-eight-inch shoulders. At the dinner table in the fo'c'sle,

Captain Vito Locrico told the crew to get some sleep after dinner, for the weather report was favorable and we would go out that night to fish for mackerel in the probably moonless night.

By 4 P.M., the last of the seiners in the fleet pulled away from the piers, and set a course toward the no man's land between Cuttyhunk and the Naushon islands.

As I lay in my bunk, a sharp pain kept me awake. The pain was between my groin and my abdomen. The pain came in waves, and sometimes I would feel like yelling out loud. Fearful of disturbing my crewmates, I went on deck and into the wheelhouse. I told the fellow on watch that I was heading for the engine room. It's too hot to sleep in the fo'c'sle, I told him.

Carl Morash, the engineer, was working on the 180 hp Cooper-Bessman direct-reversible engine. I told Carl the same story about the fo'c'sle being too hot. I was now sweating. I didn't tell Carl the truth because I thought I had just eaten too much and had cramps.

When night fell, the crew dressed in boots and oilskins and waited on deck for mackerel sightings. They noticed my absence and found me in the engine room. I said I wasn't feeling well. The boat continued its search for the telltale surface ripple of mackerel. By now, we were outside Nantucket Lightship—a lighthouse built on a ship. It was used by large freighters and steamer ships to set a true bearing for New York. The ships could bypass the shoals of Nantucket and Georges Bank on that course.

The pain came in sharp jolts, forcing me to cry out in a doubled-up position. Carl heard me and asked where I was hurting. When I showed him, he said I had appendicitis. Carl took me on deck to see Captain Locrico, who asked if the pain was serious. I told him it must be cramps from eating too much. "I'll be all right," I said. "Keep looking for the fish." He wanted to bring me in to shore.

Then Carl touched my side and I cried. Captain Locrico decided on the spot to go for New Bedford. The nearest land was eighty miles away, a nine-hour run at full throttle.

The pain would flash hot and cold as we steamed for shore. I was soaked in sweat. I was taken to the marine doctor in New Bedford. He ordered a taxi to take me and a companion from the crew to Chelsea Marine Hospital outside Boston.

The doctors operated on me the next day. It was two weeks before I could walk again and three weeks more before I'd be discharged. The federal government paid all the hospital bills. Seamen and fishermen were covered by a longstanding special act of Congress. Unfortunately, we lost that coverage during President Reagan's administration.

My "medical evacuation," if you can call it that, was a far cry from today's operations. Now hospitals send appendicitis patients home after a couple of days. Later, I heard the account of a crew member dying before receiving medical aid. A captain of another boat told me the story of his cousin who got shot accidentally while bailing fish aboard. Some sharks had made a nuisance of themselves, attacking the seine net. In the excitement of the deck work, the captain had placed the rifle against the pilot house. It discharged and hit his cousin in the stomach. The crew tried to stem the flow of blood, but when the boat reached shore six hours later, the cousin was dead.

He might have been saved today. Sophisticated communications allow fishermen to have Coast Guard boats and helicopters on the scene within minutes. Many severely injured fishermen live to tell about it today.

My second close call aboard the *Salvatore* came when the 25,000-ton luxury liner *Lafayette* made its maiden voyage to the United States.

We had made a trip of 60,000 pounds of mackerel between Block Island, Rhode Island, and no man's land, which is near Martha's Vineyard. Captain Locrico decided to land the trip at the Boston Fish Pier, figuring most of the mackerel seiners had already landed their trips in Newport or New Bedford. He was looking for a slight economic advantage in Boston by steaming through the Cape Cod Canal at night.

We were lucky to get eight cents a pound that morning. The other boats got half as much in the other ports. Boston also had the advantage of being relatively close to Gloucester and allowed for a mid-season visit to our families.

The dealer had run out of barrels as we unloaded our fish. The crew took a half-hour break. I went to the fo'c'sle for coffee and a sandwich and sat on the starboard rail, watching for the appearance of the *Lafayette*. Large crowds were watching the docking of the ship. This was something special for the city of Boston. The great ship appeared on the horizon with five tugboats and began maneuvering for Commonwealth Pier, directly across from the *Salvatore*.

Somehow the docking operation was fouled. The *Lafayette*'s forward momentum was too much. All the tugs reversed their power-ful steam engines to stop the mammoth ship from plowing into the pier's bulkhead. Finally, the *Lafayette*'s captain had no choice but to reverse the huge propellers. Otherwise, she would have made quite a dent in the pier.

Reversing the propellers in the harbor goes against every rule in the book of nautical regulations. As soon as the propellers began churning, a huge whirlpool was created and caught the tug on the

Lafayette's stern port quarter. The tug was sent hurtling at the *Salvatore*.

The captain of the tugboat tried the same maneuver as the captain of the *Lafayette*. He reversed the tug's speed full—but to no avail. It continued completely out of control. The tug smashed into the seine boat tied alongside us. The impact cut the boat in half and ripped the railing and deck planks from the *Salvatore*.

We had the seine net in the now-halved seine boat. Without thinking, I jumped from the *Salvatore*'s railing to the deck of the seine boat and grabbed the keg of the net. I guess I was thinking of saving the net, which wasn't as farfetched as it sounds, for the net was worth thousands of dollars and, more important, hours of work.

As I reached for the keg, the whirlpool from the *Lafayette* sucked the seine boat underwater—with me in it. I felt the harbor waters closing over my chest. In desperation I lashed out and caught a wooden guardrail just above the waterline of the *Salvatore*. The current pulled my body under the boat, my hands and fingernails digging into the wooden side of the *Salvatore*. Then two pairs of giant hands grabbed hold of my wrists and yanked me on deck with superhuman strength, all hundred and ninety pounds of me.

The hands belonged to my crewmates, Sebastian "Busty" Ciolino and Peter Conte, Sr. They had saved my life. Twenty minutes later, the seine boat resurfaced five hundred yards from the *Salvatore*. The corks kept the net floating.

Again, I had cheated death. The incident taught me a lesson. My attitude was this: the hell with worldly goods; your life comes first.

A *Boston Daily Record* photographer was on the scene to record the maiden voyage of the *Lafayette*. He ended up taking my picture. The caption in the next morning's newspaper read, "Rosario Testaverde was almost crushed to death" during the docking of the French liner.

I went home to Gloucester that afternoon, but not before the skipper, Vito, gave me hell. "Don't worry about a net," he said. "The insurance company will buy us a new seine boat and net, but you almost had it." I always remember him calling me foolish.

I didn't utter a word about the accident to my parents or even to my sister, who was always very close to me. I figured that no one read the Boston newspapers in Gloucester. My brother, however, read the newspapers in New Bedford, where he and the crew of the seiner *Mary W.* had landed a trip of mackerel. Peter was having his hair cut in a local barber shop when he picked up a copy of the paper and saw the picture of me being hauled out of the harbor.

Peter misread the caption, thinking it said, "Rosario Testaverde was crushed to death." He rushed out of the barber shop and telephoned Bertolino's Bakery. The baker at Bertolino's immediately got hold of my mother and brought her to the telephone. Peter blurted out the news. He was crying. My mother said he was mistaken, that I was alive and well.

Later, my sister heard the story and rushed home. When she saw me she threw her arms around me and started to cry, too. My mother joined her, crying in happiness, until I said, "what's the matter with you? I'm alive and well."

Then I got hell again. My mother told me to tell her everything that happened on the sea. I got twenty-five dollars from the insurance company for my trouble.

I continued to save two or three dollars from each trip I made on the *Salvatore*. I'd tuck my savings under the carpet. One day I counted $250 and I thought, *It won't be long before I'm driving my own car.*

It was fall again and the *Salvatore* quit seining to go dragging again down south. I was out of a job until the next seining season. I looked around on the waterfront and found a site on the seiner *Frank Wilkinson*, a World War I American subchaser converted into a fishing boat.

There were many converted subchasers in the fleet in those days. They ranged in length to 110 feet, but were only about 20 feet wide. They made good fishing boats. Frank Mineo was the captain of *Frank Wilkinson*. I made a few more dollars that fall and recounted my money. I had the same amount as three months earlier. I knew I had put at least twenty-five more away. I figured someone was fleecing it.

I moved the money into an inner pocket of a black double-breasted overcoat that I wore with a fedora. I looked like the gangster Al Capone. I took the losses and changed the hiding place.

A short time later, my mother decided to clean everything out of the closet. She wanted to air out the coats. She tipped my coat upside-down and a shower of one- and five-dollar bills fell from the pocket. She picked up the money and called for my father. He said, "It must belong to Salve; Peter makes ten dollars and spends eleven. Salve knows how to save." My money used to grow in my pocket as I walked home from the boat, my father said.

They confronted me and asked about the money. I explained that I wanted to buy a car—a Nash coupé roadster with a rumble seat. That's what I had in mind. I had girls on my mind, too.

My father had other ideas. "Salve, I know where we can get a boat cheap. It's sunk at Matthew Frontiero's wharf." I gave my father all the money and kissed the notion of a car good-bye. I had to wait thirty years before buying a battered 1958 Oldsmobile sedan.

The sunken forty-two-foot tub trawler cost fifty dollars. Peter

Favazza, the ship's chandler, had gained ownership because the previous owners had defaulted on a sizable debt.

My father, brother, and I raised our new boat by rubbing soap into the seams at low tide, when the hull was exposed and the water drained out of it. By the time the tide came back in, the boat floated.

We hired two retired marine carpenters to do the finish work. One was a tall, stooped man, Dan Fraser, who was hard of hearing, and the other we called "Pipone", which means "big pipe" in Italian. Pipone's pipe seemed always to be out and he spent quite a bit of time relighting it.

My father told Fraser and Pipone to check all the seams and planks and to repair everything underneath. They worked for a dollar and a half an hour. They also knew where to buy lumber at a cheap price. My father helped them in any way he could. I was glad for my father's sake, for now he was taking an interest in a fishing boat. He loved being his own boss. In the meantime, I went out on the *Frank Wilkinson* to support the family and help pay the bills for the boat repair.

By the end of November, the seining season was almost over and our new boat was repaired, painted, and ready to fish. My father would be at the helm and the crew consisted of myself, my brother-in-law, Lawrence, and my brother Peter. I was captain, at least according to the ownership papers. My father still couldn't own property; he was an alien until 1947. He had a wild notion of taking the whole family back to Sicily someday. My mother and all of the children disagreed with him, and there were many arguments on this subject.

On the morning of December 13, we had twenty tubs of new trawl lines prepared. That was eight miles of trawl line and 9,600 hooks. This was the maiden voyage for our new boat, the *4C555*.

We baited the hooks with frozen mackerel and traveled twenty miles east by south from Thatcher's Light to a place called Mare Nova. My father and the Boston fishermen knew this area as "New Ocean," a large fishing ground of good, hard, rocky bottom. Haddock and cod abounded here as very few dragger captains knew of these virtually virgin grounds. As we steamed into the offshore waters, the wind began to freshen from the northwest. The wind was fair, coming from behind us. These favorable conditions changed rapidly.

We overshot the grounds, turned around and headed into the wind. Now we were pounding hard to cover a mile-and-a-half distance upwind. We threw the lead overboard and made a sounding of seventy-five fathoms—too deep. We were off the edge of the bank. Finally, we reached the shoal spot, where the depth was only about forty fathoms. My father ordered us to set out the trawl line.

Nobody noticed that the bow of the boat was dipping lower and lower as we bucked up and down in the heavy seas. When my brother and I lifted the hatch cover off the fishhold, I let out a scream. Peter's scream matched mine.

We were sinking on our maiden trip. Four feet of water had the baited hooks floating in the fishhold, becoming hopelessly entangled. Everything swished back and forth peacefully. Peter and I jumped in and threw the tubs on deck. Then Lawrence, Peter and I started a bucket brigade from the fish hold to over the side. My father manned the three-inch hand pumps. We would be pumping for the next ten hours.

The floorboards were ripped away. We looked on in horror as the ocean water flowed through the opened seams. We immediately set about to caulk the seams from the inside, using a knife and some shredded cotton strips left over from the raising. We used bars of soap over the cotton. The leaks were temporarily sealed.

Lawrence went up on deck to spell my father at the pump. My father kept the bow into the wind as we moved very slowly ahead. We worked the hand pump steadily, as we knew our lives depended on saving the 4C555. We had no dory, lifeboat, or radio communications, and no other boats were in sight or in the vicinity. We were at the mercy of the sea, fighting for our lives as the wind freshened even more.

After ten hours—wet, cold, but still not tired—we reached Gloucester. God had looked kindly upon us, but we had also helped ourselves. Four things had been in our favor. First, the bulkhead wall separating the engine room from the fish hold was water tight. No water got into the engine room to drown out our motor. Second, the all-important leather thong at the end of the pump was new and refused to quit until we got home to Gloucester. (Then it tore apart and had to be replaced for fifty cents.) Third, we had a ten-pound sack of cotton waste and bars of soap to caulk the seams from the inside. And finally, our lives were at stake. Hungry and wet to the bone in the December cold, we did not tire. When we got inside Gloucester Harbor, we collapsed.

Again, we cheated death.

We took it in stride, for we had no choice. We were men of the sea. We drydocked the boat on Five Pound Island, the site of the present-day State Fish Pier, and had two French Canadian carpenters put new seams and ribs in the 4C555. The old ribs had been bent and twisted by the pounding.

It was heartbreak for us. We borrowed $350 from Peter Favazza and had the repair work done. Peter Favazza helped everybody in times of need and supplied the Italian boats. I made a point of buying three leather thongs to keep aboard as spares.

The French carpenters explained that when the boat rested under the water, mud worked into the seams, rotted the cotton and loosened the planks. When we were upwind and pounding against the seas, the cotton and mud shook free and caused the leaks.

When my father and I got hold of Dan Fraser and Pipone, we chewed the asses off them. Marine carpenters should have foreseen the damage and warned us before our setting out to sea.

I learned another rule: check the work of others. Three sons have their own boats now, and I counsel them to check all the details. Carpenters and workmen don't like it one bit when we look over their shoulders. I say it's our lives on the line when a nail gives and a plank pops open at sea. The workmen can bitch all they want to; I don't give a damn.

CAPTAIN

We had smooth sailing aboard the *4C555* after straightening out the seams. We were a family boat, one of the scores owned by Italian immigrants and crewed by sons, cousins and brothers-in-law. My own brothers, Peter, Tony and Sammy, were growing up fast and working on the boat during school vacations.

When the winter came, some of the exuberance of fishing was lost. We had a different crew and stayed a lot closer to the coast. It was hard work. We'd take the boat out in zero-degree weather. Only high winds could keep us in port. We had no choice, really; no fish meant no money. There was no unemployment compensation to fall back on; either you worked or you went hungry.

When my father and brothers fished together, I did the bulk of the heavy work, sometimes hauling as many as twelve tubs of trawl line. That allowed my father to stay at the wheel and run the engines. He was happy at the wheel. Peter was becoming a strong young man, almost as big as I was, and could haul the lines when I rested. Tony was often seasick and weak. Sammy was too young to haul yet, but he could cut and gut fish.

Sometimes, we would bring back $100 for the week. That was the total of all the shares from my father, brothers, the boat and me. We were living well now. My mother had money to put food on the table, and that was the standard for judging how well off we were.

My father and the rest of us loved to drink cold water at mealtimes. My mother would buy ten cents' worth of ice from the iceman every day to supply our old-fashioned icebox. One day I read a refrigerator advertisement in the *Gloucester Daily Times*. They were selling for $125 at North Shore Furniture Company on Main Street. I knew the store owner, Jack Levy, and made a deal with him to pay a dollar a week on the cost of the new refrigerator. I figured my mother already spent sixty or seventy cents a week on ice and agreed to make up the difference out of my pocket. I made sure everyone was home on the day it was to be delivered. We became the envy of the neighborhood. Our new Kelvinator could even make ice cubes.

"Ma, now you can throw that old icebox away," I said. "This is much better. It doesn't even need a dishpan on the floor to catch the overflow water." My father loved all the cold water that the refrigerator provided. Our food stayed fresh much longer now. In two years, it was paid for. We were buying on credit, so I guess we had finally become "Americanized."

Around this time, my mother got sick. My father worried and sometimes stayed ashore while the whole fleet was out. "Dad, let me take the boat out with my brothers," I asked. He didn't trust me yet.

We set our trawl lines one day that winter but couldn't haul them back that day because of heavy winds. My brothers, father, and I joined other frustrated fishermen on the wharves, as the winds continued. "Dad, let's go out and haul the string," I pleaded. "It's only nine miles out. If we don't take them in, we'll lose all the fish."

"No." That's all he said. That is all he felt he had to say. Two captains standing nearby shook their heads and told my father he had a crazy son. "Look how hard it's blowing," they said, almost sneering. A Boston boat rounded Harbor Cove Point and tied up in front of us. My father recognized his cousin, Nino Lauria, as the captain of this Boston boat and called him to the wharf. Nino said he'd come in because of the weather, rather than proceed to the Isle of Shoals off New Hampshire, his actual destination. They talked for about ten minutes on the wharf and then turned and walked toward our house on Commercial Street. They were still talking.

When they were out of sight, I called my brothers. "Let's go," I said. They were all willing to get in on the conspiracy.

I put Peter at the wheel. He'd steer the course and run the engines. Tony and Sammy were on deck with me. We ran out of Gloucester Harbor full-throttle and rounded Eastern Point Light. A southeasterly course took us nine miles to buoys marking our trawl lines. I hauled twelve, then switched places with Peter, who pulled the other four.

We bucked our way home through northwest winds and heavy seas. There was much spray and some ice on deck. We tied up late that evening with a trip of 6,000 pounds of mostly cod and a few haddock and cusk. Cape Ann Fisheries paid me the going rate.

When I got home, my mother said my father was worried and had been down to the wharf four times since he found out I had taken the boat out alone with just my brothers. "He's worried and just went out looking again," she said.

"Ma, we're hungry," I said. "Give us something to eat. We've been working all day. We're hungry."

Then I gave her the $120 we had earned. Her eyes opened wide and she exclaimed, "Oh, my God!"

My father came home and started giving me hell in front of my brothers. I shouldn't disobey his orders, he shouted. "Dad, I'm sixteen years old, going on seventeen. When are you going to trust me?"

My father was taken aback by the question. Then his face beamed. "Did you get any fish?" he asked in a quiet voice. Over supper we talked about the trip and the money we had made.

The wind blew from the northwest the next day and the boats again all stayed safely in port. All the other fishermen called me crazy but I laughed secretly, knowing I had pulled a fast one on them.

From that day forward, whenever my mother felt sick, I told my father to stay in and I'd take the boat out with my brothers. My father would take care of my mother. I always tried to do my best and that's how I got to be captain at only sixteen. I had a fine crew, though a little green. The total combined ages of Peter, Tony and Sammy was thirty-nine.

Nineteen thirty-four was a happy year. The family now fished together and my mother was buying things we had gone without before. We all ate much better now. But the dark side remained; my mother still was not feeling well.

Many were the nights we called Dr. Cohen or Dr. Pett. Treatment for high blood pressure was not advanced. My father would stay ashore and take care of my mother. He would do all the housework and cooking and give her companionship, for outside of the wharves, he didn't go anyplace. He was constantly by her side, something I would later do when my wife's health failed.

In the meantime, we boys took the boat out fishing, keeping the household afloat. The family fortunes improved steadily during the mid-thirties. Pauline's husband, Lawrence, never owned a boat after the *Pauline S.*, but he always had a site on one of the bigger boats that went to Georges Bank or on our family boat between offshore trips. Pauline and Lawrence were happy raising a family. Peter and I were pulling down full shares or taking the family boat out fishing. Tony and Sammy were just beginning to fish. My parents and all the boys took good care of Jimmy. Little Rosie had all the looks in the family.

I took up smoking to go along with being a captain.

A CAPTAIN'S RESPONSIBILITY

Being captain was not always such a pleasant task. In March of 1934 I got caught aboard the *4C555* during a nor'easter for nine days, and I was so bottled up I ended up smoking the whole broom.

Sammy was on that trip, to the Isles of Shoals, with Lawrence, Pepe Orlando and Pepe Favazza. Peter was away fishing off Virginia on the *St. Providenza*, a big dragger skippered by Philip Giammanco.

We baited and headed for a spot off the New Hampshire coast called the Southeaster. We set our trawl on a cool, calm afternoon and retreated into the shelter of Star Island for the night.

Before dawn the boat was shaking. We could feel the storm even as we slept on the floor of the aft cabin. I crawled out, turned up the stove and went on deck. We were anchored inside a small granite breakwater, protected from the blasting by the cluster of islands. I was surprised. There had been no hint of a storm in the skies the night before. Now look at us—bobbing up and down with every swell, sheets of rain slapping my face, the roar of the winds howling in my ears. At least we were safe in this deserted harbor. Our boat would hold; we'd keep the stove hot and wait for the weather to break. We had no choice. The Coast Guard station was less than a mile away, on Appledore Island, but we had no dory and probably wouldn't have risked a man in one, anyway. We had, of course, no radio.

Both Pepes were old men, about my father's age, in their late fifties. We fried, broiled, baked and stewed the few cod we had caught the first day; played cards, smoked cigarettes and tried to sleep. On the fifth day, however, the winds shifted to a strong gale from the northwest. Now we were getting buffeted directly through the gap between the islands. We hauled anchor and moved upwind to along-side a granite pier which was used by ferry passengers in the summer-time. The crew wanted to try for Portsmouth, but I refused. After we smoked our last cigarette, Lawrence and both Pepes really started to get on my nerves. I would not move a foot beyond the pier. I was captain and would not let the other men change my mind. Sammy added that the boat had a sorry history and probably couldn't take much of a pounding. All the discussion about Portsmouth ended.

I rigged up a spring line to save the boat from breaking up against the pier. I fastened a rope to the anchor line, heaved it ashore, and tied the boat to a piling. I ran another line from the bow to the shore. This kept the boat secure and prevented it from banging against the granite pier.

Four more days passed. I paced like a caged animal craving for a smoke. The smallest butts were unraveled and the bits of tobacco rolled up again. The Pepes chewed the same old plug of tobacco, then saved it for another chew. They gave me hell for not taking them ashore at Portsmouth.

As I was playing cards, a desperate idea took hold. I dropped my cards, eyes fixed on the cornhusk broom in the corner. I cut a little pile of straw shavings on the floor and rolled a cigarette. "Salve's flipping," said Pepe Orlando. "He's gone over the edge," said Pepe Favazza.

I offered each man my broom cigarette, but none accepted. On the tenth day, a Coast Guard launch came alongside. The officer said the station had received a boat-missing report out of Gloucester. "Who reported it missing?" I asked.

"Peter Vassar," he replied.

I knew instantly that Peter Favazza had reported us missing. Nine days out at sea; a picture of my mother and father hysterical in Bertolino's Bakery flashed into my head. They were waiting hysterically with me safe and sound and standing right in front of this officer asking me if I was lost. Now the whole family must be in week-long vigil praying for a miracle!

The Coast Guard ferried me to the station and I telephoned Peter Favazza's chandlery. "Why the hell didn't you call earlier?" he asked. I tried to explain, but it didn't matter what I said. The word went through the Fort and waterfront that we were safe and coming home.

A Coast Guardsman gave me a can of Prince Albert tobacco be-fore dropping me at the boat. The next day the winds had calmed down as we untied our lines and cleared the breakwater. There was great relief in the change of scenery. After a while, Pepe Orlando and Pepe Favazza started talking to me again. We found only four of ten markers to our trawl lines before we ran back to Gloucester. I felt pretty bad at losing half of our gear. On shore, my mother threw her arms around my neck and held tight. I told my father about the lost gear. "The hell with the gear—trawl lines can be replaced," he said; "you and your brother can't."

Opening the cod end aboard the *Linda B*. (From left to right: Joe Testaverde, Tommy Frontiero, Salve Testaverde).

Cutting pollack aboard the *Bethulia*. (From left to right: Thomas Lupo, Salve Testaverde, Nicky Curcuru, Ambrose Orlando, Tommy Curcuru).

Salve Testaverde and Joe Orlando aboard the *Bethulia*.

Crew on the *Bethulia* showing a moola-moola or sunfish (From left to right: Vincent Nicastro, Salve Testaverde, Ambrose Orlando, Pepino Curcuru, Sam Curcuru, Libbey Curcuru, John Curcuru, Nick Curcuru).

Salve Testaverde hauling trawl line at age 16.

Splitting the bag aboard the *Sea Fox*.

Deck full of cod and ling aboard the *Sea Fox*.

Aboard the *Sea Fox*: Crew man Joe Curcuru mending the cod end, thus saving a catch of 25,000 pounds of ling and whiting.

Hand Lining.

Gill Netting.

Purse Seining.

Side Trawling.

NINA

In the fall of 1934, I was an usher, matched with Lena Randazza at her sister's wedding at St. Ann's Church. She was my godmother's daughter but we had never met, even though we lived less than 150 feet away from each other. Her parents were *compari* to mine. Every pew was filled with the families of the Fort.

Without realizing it then, I was drawn into a very formal courtship. When Joe Scola and Bessie Mione got married the following year, "Nina" and I were matched again. Nobody consulted me about it and I certainly didn't mind. I liked being with her.

I had never had time for girls. Where did you meet girls? I had not been to school for four years. I had grown up with only my family and other fishermen. The only chance was at weddings, it seemed.

When Bessie and Joe Scola returned from their honeymoon, they hosted a party for all the wedding attendants. I had something to drink in the kitchen and joined everyone for a game in the living room. Each player had to draw a slip of paper and act out its command or pay a forfeit. When it was my turn, I became embarrassed at the command: "Make believe you are Romeo and propose to your Juliet." I handed it to a friend to read it aloud while everyone jeered and whistled.

With a few drinks under my belt, my eyes sparkled as I gazed at Nina. She covered her mouth with a hand and flew out of the room. The girls followed her into the kitchen and brought her back. She was seated on a chair in the middle of the room and I knelt on one knee in front of her. "I like you and I know you like me," I said. "I think I'm going to send my mother to see your mother during Christmas."

In those days, the families managed everything. If Nina's family would accept me, we could be engaged. If not, I would not even be allowed in her house. The tradition was strong and well known to everyone.

When Christmas came, our parents met and I was told by my mother to give Nina a friendship ring. My pal, Tom ("Jack Brady") Randazza, Nina's brother, told his mother, "Mom, grab him. Hold on to him. Salve's a good kid."

At first, I had to take Nina's two married sisters to the North Shore Theater for dates with her. It reminded me of having two seine boats alongside. Her mother would name the hour and minute we were to return. After a month and a half, I protested and had a loud argument with her one night. "If you don't trust me with Nina, then I can't have anything to do with you," I told her and walked out of the apartment. Nina's mother relented, the romance resumed and four years later we were married. It took that long to save up enough money to buy furniture.

I had gotten a site on board the *Bethulia*, captained by Phil Curcuru. The captain's son was my *compare*, Salvatore. The *Bethulia* was a 74-foot converted yacht. She proved able in all weather, including the killer hurricane of 1938. During my four seining seasons on the *Bethulia*, many deep friendships took root, and Nina and I stood up as bridesmaid and usher at more weddings, including Antoinette Aiello and Frank Militello's, where we served as best man and maid of honor.

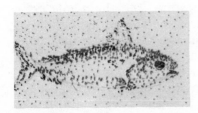

THE *BETHULIA*

The 1938 mackerel season was storm after storm, ending with the Great Hurricane in September. I was fishing with the *Bethulia* that year, still with Captain Philip Curcuru. The captain's brother, Joseph ("Pepino") Curcuru, who co-owned the boat, worked on deck with his stepbrother, Salvatore ("Snake") Nicastro, the twinesman. Joe Peep had come over from the *Maria Concetta* and was engineer. Ambrose Orlando was cook; Big John Aiello, the mastman; and Vito Giacalone and I, the dorymen. Vincenzo Nicastro was corksman aboard the seine boat; Tommy Lupo the lead linesman; and Matteo LoGrande, another twinesman. Joe Pepino's young son Sammy and the captain's boys, Tommy and Nicky, were also aboard and worked in the seine boat.

It was around the middle of May when we were fishing out of New York at the "gully." The gully was about eighty miles offshore near where the continental shelf ends in the Atlantic. The entire fleet was anxious because we had all been in port for nearly a week on account of the high winds. This day the seas were calm and the air still. We reached the gully during mid-afternoon and lay to waiting for nightfall to fish. Most of the fleet was already there.

After several hours of waiting, we noticed one of the American boats, the *Eleanor*, making the rounds to the other boats. Its captain, "Lem " Firth, was obviously carrying a message. When he got to us, he warned of hearing about southeast gales which had been forecast on his radio. Captain Phil appreciated the news but decided to stay. So did the *Beatrice & Rose*, captained by Jerome Frontiero. The rest of the fleet steamed north for shelter in either New Bedford or Block Island. In those days, although most of the Italians didn't have radios, some of the American skippers, like Lem, listened for everyone.

As the sun set the wind slackened. If anything, it seemed as if the weather was getting better, not worse. The first clouds came an hour later just as we started to fish. It wasn't long after dusk that John Aiello spotted our first fish from the crosstrees, and the whole crew was quick to set out. On our first set we had the fish in the middle of the seine, right where we wanted them, but lost them when they dove underneath the lead line before we could purse the seine. Fishing involves a good bit of skill, but you can't succeed without some luck.

As we hauled back, the winds began to freshen, and without much notice, it was blowing twenty knots and the seas were beginning to chop. As a precaution, Captain Phil ordered the net onto the stern deck, in case we lost control of the seine boat. By the time the net was stowed, it was blowing hard and raining in sheets as we cursed our luck.

Less than half a mile away, the *Beatrice & Rose*, lit up like a Christmas tree, was bailing 25,000 pounds of the mackerel that we had missed. We stopped to talk—or shout—briefly as we passed. We were now steaming to Block Island with our seine boat in tow.

After several hours of running with the wind and the waves at our starboard beam, the storm had reached gale force and our seine boat was slowly sinking into the ocean. Captain Phil brought the *Bethulia* to a halt and we lay to as we scrambled on deck to rescue the boat. At first, we heaved and pulled on the towline, three inches thick and nearly five hundred feet long. It was tough pulling because of all the water in the seine boat. As we got it within reach, each wave threatened to ram the half-sunken seine boat right through the *Bethulia* like a torpedo. By now the seas were running twenty feet. More work, and we were all soaked and scared. Once the seine boat was alongside, we were still not safe because now as each wave crashed at and over the siderails, the seine boat almost came with it. The captain ordered the line loose. We were nearly useless, beating our heads and bodies against the ocean, which showed no signs of letting up on us. One after the other, the waves came. Each one was bigger than the one before. Somebody, I'm not sure who, suggested we launch the dory and get the seine boat that way. I knew that Tommy Lupo, Snake Nicastro and I would be chosen to row. I didn't like the idea and said so. "The minute we get into the dory, we'll capsize. If you think it's such a great idea, you get in first and I'll be right behind you."

At that, the captain took charge again and ordered the dory back to its cradle. "Get the grappling hook; make up another line," he hollered. The captain wanted two lines on the seine boat, one in the bow and one astern. Snake made several throws with the hook and finally caught onto the stern. The whole crew tugged at both lines until the seine boat was close but still heaving up and down with each wave. It was as close as we could get it. The moment was here. It was time to jump: the three of us, Tommy, Snake and me. If you missed, you could die, either crushed between the two hulls or drowned. Standing at the rail, hugging the rigging, I was scared stiff. Later, Snake and Tommy told me they had the same frightening thoughts. In rapid succession, though, we each made it.

In the seine boat, the three of us took turns hand-pumping all that water until the bilge was dry. We tightened the four six-volt bulbs we had for night-lights that had become loose, so that when we started to run again or steam, we would have visibility. We made sure everything was in order and shouted to the rest of the crew to pull us in again, taking our chances on jumping aboard the boat again, a dangerous job. We made it, obviously. When we were aboard, we shouted to the captain to go half-speed ahead, and Vincenzo Nicastro played out the slack on the rope line. A huge wave came crashing down on us, suddenly thrusting the *Bethulia* away from the seine boat and momentarily freeing the line away from Vincenzo and the other crew. Now the seine boat was adrift, upwind from us about twenty feet, when in the next instant it was on the crest of the next wave, and with all that slack line in the water. The propeller kept turning ahead and caught the rope, cutting it in two, the short end going to the seine boat and the rest to us on the *Bethulia*, now drifting away with the wrong end.

The results were disabling. With the gale and all, Peppino Curcuru got excited and started to wail. Bad enough we lost the seine boat; now we were going to lose our lives. Captain Phil told him to calm down. Sizing up the situation, he gave orders to Joe Peep to put the clutch in neutral and stop the engine, get the big Stillson wrench, and turn the shaft counterclockwise on his orders. He also ordered two of the crew and his brother to go down in the engine room and help Joe.

Meanwhile, the rest of the crew on deck got hold of the rope that was trailing over the side to the wheel, and on the captain's orders, we started pulling with all our strength. The *Bethulia* was lying dead still now and the waves came crashing over the sides engulfing us. Everyone was trying to hang on for dear life; the deck was awash with two feet of water. As the boys below turned the shaft, we pulled and felt it give, and as they kept turning, the rope came free from the propeller. We were safe, at least for the moment.

The skipper climbed back to the wheelhouse and began to

maneuver the boat downwind to search for the drifting seine boat. In doing so, a huge wave came crashing down on us, rolling us over and listing us badly. The big pile of seine net shifted across the deck, pinning young Sammy against the port rail. He was screaming with fright because he couldn't move, but he wasn't hurt. We didn't know that then. Seeing him pinned, we all feared the worst: crushed legs. His father shouting directions, we all got on the side of the net and pushed with all our might, when the boat itself rolled over to starboard, freeing his legs. Sammy wasn't hurt, just scared.

In the meantime, going downrange with the wind behind us, we spotted the lights of the seine boat in all that rain. We were lucky as quite a bit of time had passed with all the mishaps. Getting the grappling hook, we went alongside the seine boat, grabbing it again, struggling to hold her. Tommy, Snake and I risked our lives again. We tied the three-inch parted rope together with a square knot, and once that was done, the same danger returned, getting aboard the mother vessel.

We were wet, still scared and cold, as we headed for Block Island. The captain ordered that nobody was to go down in the forecastle. Four men lined up in the pilothouse, taking turns steering, and the rest of the crew stayed behind the house, crouching low and watching the seine boat astern of us.

Later, when we got into port, I asked the captain why he kept us on deck aft, instead of ordering some of us into the fo'c'sle down forward. He gave me this answer. "This boat is old, and in case something happens, I don't want to see anybody trapped below." In later years, one of my boats was in a similar situation, and I kept the crew with me in the wheelhouse, together, giving each other courage.

Just before dawn, we spotted a light in the distance. The rain and wind had let up but the seas were mountainous. Going toward the light, we recognized it as a buoy, but what buoy? We didn't know. Staying a distance away from it, we waited for daylight and better visibility. All we had aboard was a compass. We had none of today's navigational equipment, and these seiners traveled hundreds of miles up and down the coast. You have to give credit to those old-time captains, some of whom didn't even know how to read or write.

As daylight approached, we saw that we were on the southeast side of Block Island. We shifted course and steamed to the New Harbour on the northwest side, where we found five of the boats that had been with us at the gully. We tied up at the dock, everyone tired and wet. We all turned in for a much-needed rest, after facing danger all night in that storm. And without making one cent. Such were the breaks in this fishing business.

Awakening much later, we found out that the Block Island Coast

Guard had clocked this storm at sixty-five miles per hour. Two boats that got caught in it lost their seine boats. The practice of putting the seine on deck whenever it got windy saved many nets on these mackerel vessels.

That fall the *Bethulia* and crew were involved with helping the Gloucester Coast Guard and the fire department in the rescue mission of a fishing-party boat on the Annisquam River. It was during the Great Hurricane of 1938. That's just another story that went unreported. If old fishermen would only open up and talk, many a story they could tell.

FIESTA

Fishermen have always revered St. Peter as their patron saint. Around 1930, Captain Salvatore Favazza, with his own money, purchased a statue of St. Peter in Italy and arranged to have it shipped to Gloucester. When the statue arrived, it brought a tremendous response from everyone in the Fort. It was nearly five feet high, beautifully carved and painted, with penetrating eyes and uplifted heart, with a great likeness to the pictures we had all grown up seeing in our houses and in our churches. It was first publicly displayed in a vacant lot opposite the Griffin Coal Company, at the end of Commercial Street.

Within hours, all the women in the Fort came out with their best bedspreads and hung them against the side wall of the Favazza store and over the statue, forming a canopy. They also brought candles, incense and flowers with them and built a makeshift altar. Chairs were circled around and rosaries were prayed and ancient Sicilian chants were sung. A priest came and blessed the statue. In the crowd there were women of all ages, young and old, bound together by a tradition and a hope for better times and fortunes. The men stood by watching, sipping wine and talking.

The first fiesta was not organized like the ones today. Vito Mione, the "town crier" of the Fort, banged his drums and marched up and down the street, yelling, *"Yamo, yamo, alistamino, comagia, la festa comincia."* "Come, come, hurry up (one, two, three), come, the fiesta is about to start." Soon everyone was in the streets and at the statue. Sebastian Lovasco quickly organized a series of foot and sack races for the kids. Soon other people were playing games, some of which had not been played for years. One I remember involved a soot-blackened frying pan hanging from a rope. In the pan there was a coin. The trick was to get the coin out of the pan using only your teeth, with your hands tied behind your back. Each time the pan moved, your face got dirtier and more people laughed. For my efforts, I once got fifty cents.

Within a few years there were the dory and seine boat races and a greasy pole event, not like the one we have today, but a vertical greasy pole on land. Bands became common after the boat owners and crews began supporting the Fiesta with some money. Later on, Gloucester businesses and citizens sent donations.

By the late thirties, the St. Peter's Fiesta attracted ranking state politicians among its crowd of thousands. Rollicking sporting events were traditional arenas for young men to make a name. The greasy pole event was just that—a thirty-foot greased pole, twenty-five feet over the water, with a red pennant attached to the end. A young man was to walk the pole and leap at the pennant as he fell to the water. The man who got the flag was the hero, but those who missed provided an afternoon's lighthearted drama on Pavilion Beach.

The seine boat races were taken more seriously. Here was a chance for a young fishermen to prove his brawn and skill at moving a forty-two-foot boat over a one-mile course. Each seine boat—the *Salvatore*, the *Bethulia*, the *Antonina*—put a ten-man team in the field. In 1935, the battleship *Tennessee*, anchored off Gloucester, sent a team of oarsmen to race against the best of the fishermen and lost.

I took my chances on the greasy pole and rowed each summer until the war interrupted the fiesta. The fiesta of 1938 was hard for me to take. My younger brothers, Peter, Tony and Sammy, rowed for the winning team, edging out the *Bethulia* crew, and their older brother, by three lengths. I got a lot of grief for losing to my "little" brothers, but took it well, saying they won only because they had a lighter boat. Actually, my brothers were full-grown men in their teens, and I was very proud of them. After they shipped out to Normandy and Iwo Jima three years later, I worried every day.

The most exciting seine boat races were in 1939. The battleship *Arkansas* called at Gloucester and happened to have a team of crack Annapolis midshipmen aboard to issue a challenge. Mayor Sylvester Whalen went aboard the *Arkansas* to accept the challenge for the fishermen. Preliminary races were called on Pavilion Beach. I put every ounce of muscle I had into the oars to make the team, along with my brother Peter, who was just as big as me, Tommy Lupo, Sam ("Tally") Nicastro, Peter ("Petdetz") Frontiero, ("Kelly") Frontiero, Sam ("Red Top") Curcuru, Salvatore ("Tootsie") Parisi, Snake Nicastro and John Parisi, the coxswain.

The Annapolis crew trained for a week before the race. We stood on the street corner and watched as they ran in *NAVY* sweatsuits along Stage Fort Park and the waterfront. They even did calisthenics in Newell Stadium.

"What a waste of time," we muttered. Secretly, I was thinking they looked like football players; they were awfully big. When they trained in the boats, we carefully counted their strokes per minute. Our training consisted of resting. We rowed for a living, not as a game.

The Gloucester and Boston newspapers had stories about the race in their sports sections. A great crowd lined the beach and the back porches of the Fort when the gun fired and both boats shot away. We had a half mile to the pennant, around the buoys, and a half mile back to the beach. We made three strokes to their two and pulled away. At the turn, we had three lengths on them. We never let up on our pace and won by five lengths.

The beach went wild. People were grabbing and hugging each other, tumbling into the surf with excitement. When we got the boats back to Town Landing in the heart of the Fort, Mayor Whalen was waiting there with a couple of cases of beer and a bottle of whiskey. The celebration continued across the street at the St. Peter's Club bar. The Navy rowers met up with us there and made excuses about their loss. "We weren't used to the seine boats," they complained.

"Okay, we'll race you in your own boats," someone offered, "tomorrow."

"You're on."

The people came out to the waterfront again for the grudge match. The Navy men rowed out to the beach in their sleek, lightweight whale boats. As we practiced, we shortened our strokes even more. Stroke, stroke, stroke, quick bursts of strength.

The gun sounded and we dug hard. This time we embarrassed the Navy by almost ten lengths. The beach exploded with screams, whistles and horns. A Navy officer called for quiet and made a little speech. "These are hardworking, powerful men of the sea," he said. "They have earned our everlasting respect."

In the confusion of the great celebration, I had missed Nina. I wanted her on my arm when I paraded around the Fort and went to the St. Peter's Club. I finally found her at her mother's house. "I'm very proud of you," she said with a kiss.

The headlines of the *Gloucester Daily Times* the next day read: "Fishermen Defeat Navy Oarsmen." We had made quite a splash. I was relieved the Navy never challenged us at five miles. They would have swamped us at any distance races.

The seine boats had another competition among themselves, this one worth more money than prestige. The mackerel season usually ended in late November or early December. The fish simply disappeared. The captain who could find and land a trip of mackerel in December was handsomely paid. The crew that landed the last trip of the season earned a bonus and bragging rights. In 1938, the seiner *Santa Maria* astounded the rest of the fleet by landing a trip in early January. The *Bethulia* was the runner-up. We had changed over our nets for dragging under the impression that the *Santa Maria* had also stripped its seining gear. The highest price ever paid for mackerel went to the crew of the *Santa Maria* while the crew of the *Bethulia* was having trouble finding groundfish for dragging.

The next winter's catch was the *Bethulia*'s. Frigid weather kept all but the most hardy seiners in port in late December. By New Year's Day, only five boats were still seining. On January 17, the *Bethulia* landed 72,000 pounds of mackerel in New Bedford. Five days later, we came in with the season's final catch—42,000 pounds. We had the new record. Our bonanza brought $435 to each crew member.

When I got home to Gloucester, I rushed up the backstairs to the kitchen of our apartment. "Ma, Ma! Count it," I said, handing my mother a big roll of bills. "Count it!"

She counted the hundred-dollar bills as tens. She had never seen a bill higher than that. I held one up before her eyes. "Ma, this is worth ten ten-dollar bills," I said.

THE WAR

Nina Randazza and I exchanged wedding vows at St. Ann's Church on January 27, 1940. I was twenty-two and she was twenty. We had been engaged for more than four years, but I had put off the marriage until I had $1,200 in savings. After I bought our furniture and paid all the wedding bills, including our honeymoon at the Parker House in Boston, Nina and I had forty dollars left.

We made our home in a three-room apartment on Pascucci Court, not far from our parents' houses in the Fort. When we returned home from the honeymoon, Nina served me ham and scrambled eggs at every meal for three days straight. On the fourth day, I begged her to cook something, anything, else.

"I don't know how to cook anything else," she cried, bursting into tears. I was stunned and I sent her to my mother and sister. I was afraid I'd starve to death. They gave Nina a crash course in cooking for my healthy appetite. After that, Nina would cook all the time. In less than a year, she was cooking as well as my mother and I was happy to sit down to dinner.

The winter of 1940 was hard and mean. Northeast gales and blizzards of snow pounded us. I had left the *Bethulia* for tub trawling aboard the little *4C555* with my father and brothers. Somehow, Nina and I managed to get by on my meager wages. I was always broke, but at least the bills got paid.

When foul weather kept the boat tied up for three straight weeks, I finally swallowed my pride and took my first—and only—shoreside job. I earned forty cents an hour cutting blocks of ice from Fernwood

Lake in West Gloucester. I worked with Phil Harvey. The ice was stored in a warehouse next to the lake. I enjoyed the physical exertion of the work. In my heart I knew I was meant to have a salty breeze in my face and the ocean below my feet. Between ice-cutting jobs, I also strung herring in Slade Gorton's smokehouse. I worked onshore for only a month.

When spring finally arrived, I got a site on the seiner *Antonina*, captained by Nina's cousin, Benny Randazza. Two of Nina's brothers-in-law and two cousins were also aboard the boat. I started to see good money now, very good money. Mackerel was fetching seven cents a pound from the "big three" processors on the Gloucester waterfront: Gorton-Pew Fisheries, Davis Brothers, and Progressive Fish Company. The processors bought all the fish we landed and wanted more. Our mackerel catches helped feed the European allies in the war and the U.S. government kept the price stable. I think it was all part of Roosevelt's Lend-Lease program.

That fall, however, I quit the *Antonina* to go aboard the *Rosie and Lucy*, which could be changed over from seining to dragging according to the season. Captain Phil Parisi and his brother/co-owner Lawrence Rubino were a pair of good men. They always watched out for the welfare of the crew, and I respected them for that. They were real gentlemen, not like some of the Turks I'd seen around.

It was about at this time that the federal government came out with strict new regulations for fishing boats. We wouldn't enter the war for almost another year, but the government was busy making way for it, long before Pearl Harbor.

The government considered the waterfront a strategic area and required all fishermen to have identification cards with photographs. I still have mine at home. The Coast Guard cracked down on boats without registration numbers painted clearly on the bows, sides and even on the pilothouse roofs. Boats were often stopped for routine inspections.

Heavily armed English and Canadian navy ships suddenly appeared off the New England coast. They were assigned to escort merchant and supply convoys across the Atlantic to our allies. Sometimes more than a hundred ships gathered in a single convoy. Seen from the deck of a fishing boat, the convoys made an extraordinary sight as ship after ship made its way out of Boston Harbor or through the Cape Cod Canal. Never had I seen so many ships together at once. At night they all ran without lights.

Military operations in our waters made fishing all the more dangerous, especially at night or in the fog. When the convoys were nearby, we kept our decks blacked out. We were afraid of attracting the attention of some trigger-happy gunman aboard one of the escort ships. We didn't want anyone firing first and asking questions later.

We lived with the risk of being run down by a convoy. The big ships and tankers carrying supplies to the allies weren't able to change their courses to avoid a little fishing boat. It was the responsibility of the fishing boat's captain to stay clear of these giant ships. On many nights, the faint silhouette of a convoy in the distance determined our course.

When a fishing boat became caught in a fog bank, lookouts had to be posted on every quarter of the deck to watch for the convoys. Fog was much more dangerous than nightfall, because at least the skipper could predict the hour of nightfall and plan for it. Fog came at any hour. My worst fog and convoy adventure was aboard the seiner *Rosie and Lucy* after the war actually started. The crew had just completed a tow when a Canadian navy ship loomed out of the fog next to us.

"Clear out this area," the Canadian captain shouted into the bullhorn. "This is a restricted area. A convoy is coming through." We turned to starboard and suddenly the bow of a ship appeared in our path. We turned to port and another hulking bow appeared. These 500-foot ships dwarfed our eighty-six-foot seiner. Captain Parisi and crew became rattled as the *Rosie and Lucy* swung one way, then the other, to stay ahead of the charging ships.

We didn't mind dodging one ship—but this was ridiculous. There must have been 150 ships out there. The whole crew was scared to death. We finally managed to outrun the convoy at full throttle, and headed home for Gloucester Harbor. Radar would save a future generation of fishermen from this kind of aggravation and fright. For the time being, we had to rely on instinct, eyesight and good luck.

No amount of new technology could save us from our greatest dread—sinking by German submarines. The Germans had already said they would sink any escort vessels off our coast. We feared being mistaken for a military vessel. Some Gloucester boats were sunk.

One that I remember was the boat *Ben and Josephine*, captained by Joe Ciaramitaro. In 1942 the Germans shelled his boat as he was steaming toward the Western Hole off Nova Scotia. The crew, fortunately, escaped in dories and spent more than thirty-six hours rowing before they made land near Mt. Desert Island on the Maine coast. All Gloucester fishermen lived with the fear that their boats might be next.

In December, 1941, the *Rosie and Lucy* was mackerel fishing south of Cape Cod. We had landed a trip in New Bedford and were given a day off. Captain Parisi and the crew all took the bus home to Gloucester. While at home, we heard the news about Pearl Harbor. We were stunned. No more half-measures. The United States was in the war against Japan.

After a couple of days in Gloucester, the crew took the Boston and Maine train back to New Bedford. Navy guards challenged us at the pier. When we showed our identification cards, we were allowed to pass.

The weather was poor, so we stayed aboard the boat, in port. We were afraid to go ashore. Would the guards allow us back aboard the *Rosie and Lucy*? There was great confusion.

On December 10, the *Rosie and Lucy* untied its lines and set out for the fishing grounds. At 6 A.M., just as we were clearing New Bedford Harbor, a bulletin came over the radio that Germany and Italy had declared war on the United States.

Now we were really feeling down in the dumps. Every one of us had relatives in Italy. We were loyal Americans, but we anguished over the fate of our relatives back in our mother country. We plotted a course for fishing grounds outside Block Island, just doing our jobs. Our spirits were very low. Our cousins, brothers, sisters, and in some instances, even wives were now the enemy.

Before we got to fish, the wind freshened up from the southwest and the captain decided to head for the shelter of Block Island. We were greeted immediately in the harbor by three jeeps of Coast Guardsmen dressed in combat fatigues, carrying rifles and sidearms. They looked ready for action. The bosun's mate ordered Captain Parisi to have the crew line up on deck. After inspecting our papers, the Coast Guardsmen herded us into jeeps and drove us to the Coast Guard station. I felt like a prisoner of war.

The crews of the seiners *Santa Maria* and *Serafina N.* were already being held in the basement of the station. Only the captains and first mates were allowed to stay with the boats. Everybody else waited, about forty men cramped into a little room with only two small windows for light and air. "What the hell's going on?" we asked the guards. All we got was a two-word reply: "Keep quiet."

Eventually, we settled into playing cards or sleeping on the cement floor. We were there all day and time dragged. I asked permission to go to the head and a guard led me away and stood sentry outside. "Hey, I'm an American citizen, you know," I told him; "I was born in this country. What the hell is wrong?"

"You'll find out in due time," he said. "Now hurry up." After seven hours, the guards finally brought us hot dogs and beans, sliced bread and butter, and some soft drinks. They dragged some old car seats with springs downstairs for us.

An hour later, the guards started to call out names. One by one, the men disappeared. Nobody came back. Nobody said anything as we wondered what was going on upstairs. Were men being shot? There we sat, in the dark, being led away one by one. Finally, thank

God, my name was called and the guard led me upstairs to a big office furnished with a huge desk and a map of the United States.

A navy officer, an army officer, and a civilian in a business suit, without even telling me their names, started asking me a lot of questions about my family. Where were they born? How long had they been in this country? Did they work? Did they have family and friends in Italy? Did I have any brothers? Sisters? Where were they born?

I answered every question they fired at me. The civilian was probably an FBI agent; he had official records in front of him to make sure my answers were accurate. "My mother's been in this country since 1916 and my father's been here longer," I said. "I was born here. Why are you treating me like a prisoner of war?"

"We're checking out everyone," said the civilian. Actually they were looking for illegal aliens working aboard the boats. Before, it had been illegal for aliens to own a boat. Now it was illegal for aliens to even work aboard the boats. We had one illegal on our boat, but Captain Parisi put up a bond for his release. It cost $500 and took three days to arrange for his release while the rest of us waited on board. Other captains may have left, but not Phil Parisi.

I felt my rights had been violated. When I read about the Japanese Americans forced into internment camps on the West Coast, I kept my protests to myself.

My father and father-in-law, Salvatore Randazza, and Lawrence Rubino and many other good people of Gloucester were aliens. They had never applied for U.S. citizenship despite living in this country for years. Some clung to the dream of returning to the old country. Others were just too lazy or stubborn to change citizenship. In any case, these men were prohibited from fishing or even working in the fish-cutting plants on the waterfront. It wasn't until 1944 that the government relaxed the ban and allowed Italian aliens to work as stevedores—"lumpers"—unloading the boats in port.

It was a touchy situation. The government seemed very suspicious of my parents, yet three of their sons—Peter, Tony and Sammy volunteered for the navy and all served with honor.

In the midst of all the war talk and preparation, on November 13, 1940, Nina went into labor with our first son, John. I paced the Addison Gilbert Hospital corridors for nine hours before the doctor told me I was the father of a nine-pound, three-ounce baby. Then I was walking six feet off the ground. I couldn't have been happier.

OUR OWN WARS

Work aboard the *Rosie and Lucy* was too good for me to leave offshore dragging for the family boat. I was collecting $100 for trips now. Sometimes we made $300 each on a single trip. For less than a week's work, this was top dollar. I really didn't have to think twice about the old *4C555*. My brothers were gone and my father ashore. Could I let her lie idle at the dock?

I asked $500 for her, all the gear included. It was a good price, as the war had created a seller's market. Everything, particularly a money-earning small business such as the *4C555*, was in great demand. I gave the money to my parents, but my father refused. "It was your money that bought that boat in the first place." I couldn't keep the money. "Here, take it," I said. "Buy some food. You need it more than I do."

Every time we made a good trip, I'd give fifty or more dollars to my mother. I told her never to say anything to Nina. She told Nina everything, however. She simply couldn't lie. For years the two of them let me think I had a secret. I was in no way being unique or heroic in doing this for my parents. I had no choice. Was I going to let them starve?

My mother became very sick in the summer of 1942. A stroke left her paralyzed on one side and partially mute and deaf. She couldn't walk. It was always touch and go as to whether she was going to make it. All the while she worried terribly about her sons, in both the Atlantic and Pacific war zones.

Many a night we sent for the priest to give Mama the last rites, the family always keeping a solemn vigil. Somehow, she always managed to pull through the next day. Mama's health also put more of a strain on my father and me as the medical and hospital bills mounted over the next two years.

As the fall seining season came to an end, the *Rosie and Lucy* switched over to dragging, leaving me out of a job once again. That didn't last for long. I shipped out aboard the *Jennie and Lucia*, a ninety-foot dragger captained by Joseph Brancaleone and owned by Salvatore Susanno, the father-in-law of my brothers Peter and Sammy. Yes, it seemed we're all related by either blood or marriage.

Dragging was something new for me. When I encountered this modern method of fishing, recalling all the years of longline trawling, my head shook in disgust. "What a waste of time," I told my father. "All those years we worked like jackasses, catching one fish at a time, when the modern draggers catch thousands of pounds of fish in one swoop."

I was determined to learn everything about dragging. I asked questions and watched everything happening on deck with fascination. I worked hard because I had a dream. I dreamed of having my own boat again—a family boat with my sons as crew. The birth of my second son, Salvatore, on November 16, 1942, encouraged me to work even harder at fulfilling this vision.

I stayed aboard the *Jennie and Lucia* until the federal government stepped in and took the boat away. It was just like that. One morning we got the word from Captain Joe that the *Jennie and Lucia* would be used as a patrol boat off the New England coast for the remainder of the war. The government was strapped for boats of her size.

Scores of boats were expropriated by the government, staffed by the navy, and stationed outside the entrance of all the major ports. The government took many good fishing boats in this fashion. After the war ended, the boats were returned to their owners, who had been reimbursed with cash. Some boats were never returned, winding up instead in Greece, as part of the Truman Doctrine.

I remember many times being boarded by the navy personnel as we traveled from port to port. We had to carry specially issued identification cards, and the navy security crew checked our faces carefully against the ones on our cards. If that wasn't enough, the captain also had to give the correct code letters, provided daily by the navy as we left port. We would spell out the code letters by raising the colored code flags on the mainmast.

Sometimes we had to wait outside the harbor with fish aboard because of the mines. Convoys always got top priority. We had to wait two days sometimes. Three or four boats were sunk by enemy fire from submarines. We had to keep a record of every drop of fuel we burned, because some fishermen were suspected of giving German submarines fuel oil and food. That was the reason for all the restrictions.

After the *Jennie and Lucia* was taken, I shipped aboard the *Ave Maria*, a 75-foot dragger captained and owned by my *compare* Salvatore Curcuru. I made my first trip to Brown's Bank, more than 200 miles from Gloucester, off the coast of Nova Scotia, on the *Ave Maria*. It was a twenty-hour run, but the haddock were plentiful there. The eastern and western sides of the bank—the holes—were plentiful in cod, pollack and redfish. Marketing experts have since renamed redfish "ocean perch." I guess it has more appeal that way.

The *Ave Maria* also took to the southern fisheries. We'd drag off the coast of Virginia and North Carolina and land our trips in Norfolk, Virginia.

The greatest hardship in this fishing was being away for three months at a crack. I missed my family and parents. I always missed my family and looked forward to returning to my wife and sons.

One penalty of staying away from home for more than ten days was that my sons, Johnny and Salvatore, were growing up fast without me. They didn't always recognize me when I returned. They'd cry when their dad came near them, and that bothered me. Nina had to be both father and mother to the children. It was always the same for me: hit port, take out the fish and, the next day, go again. The children grew up without a father. I had no time for them. We couldn't go together to a circus or a football game because I was always out fishing. Finally, years later, I got my own boat and things changed. I had time for my sons, for they were my crew.

In Gloucester, my parents would occasionally receive a letter from one of my three brothers in the navy. Peter was in Casablanca getting ready for the invasion of Sicily. Tony was in the Pacific: New Guinea, the Carolines, the Philippines and Formosa. Sammy was part of the D-Day invasion of Normandy. Later, he was shipped to the Pacific for the invasion of Okinawa.

There was something strange about being ashore now. I think it was the absence of young men. There were few men my age on the streets.

During all these uncertain war years, my mother's worrying about her sons took its toll. Her health had steadily deteriorated until, by D-Day, she was under a doctor's constant care.

In Phoebus, Virginia, an incident occurred that today I think of as amusing and comical but at the time was anything but. We'd had engine trouble on the *Ave Maria*. After hauling up on Moonship Marine Railyard in Norfolk for tail shaft trouble, we found out it was a damaged shaft. We had two weeks to kill while the boat remained out of the water.

Being broke and sick and tired of looking at the same boats in the same shipyard, Jerome Loiacano, the cook, and I decided to ask Captain Salvatore Curcuru for a loan of ten dollars for a show in Hampton.

Captain Salvatore not only agreed to make the loan, but decided to come along with us. We went to Hampton for the movie and then headed for Phoebus, where I knew a good restaurant and bar. The three of us ordered a light snack and a bottle of beer each. The place was full of servicemen and servicewomen. We had just finished eating a sandwich when a tipsy navy WAVE came to our table and sat right down next to me. I don't know what she saw in me, but she grabbed my collar and said, "Hi, big boy."

Before I could react, and much to my embarrassment, she kissed me full on the lips. I tried to hold her off, but the damage was done. Then I took out a handkerchief and wiped my lipstick-smeared face.

The WAVE's boyfriend, a big sailor, approached us from across the bar. He was angry after seeing her kissing me. I don't know if the navy woman was trying to make her boyfriend jealous, but I do know he wanted to pick a fight with me. I tried to reason with him, but then he started to insult me. Still, my companions and I kept our cool, for now all the ser-vicemen in the bar had formed a big ring around the table. I kept cool, figuring that if I hit him, Jerome, Captain Salvatore and I would be clobbered.

The servicemen asked why I wasn't in uniform and why I wasn't fighting for the war effort. I told them that we were commercial fishermen taking our chances on the open sea against enemy submarines, to help supply the armed forces with fish.

When the servicemen heard this, they took the sailor and his girlfriend away. Thus, a fight was averted.

Or at least for the time being.

We left the bar and got a taxi back to the boat in Norfolk. We had come close to getting a beating. Below deck, I undressed and put my dark blue suit back in the suitcase and stowed it away.

A week later, the engine part and shaft arrived, the boat was repaired, and we fished again. We made one small trip. With all the time lost on repairs, Captain Salvatore decided to head for Gloucester. He had received a weather report that gale winds were coming from the southwest and the fish were again off the coast of New England. With the gale winds behind us, we arrived in Gloucester in less than two days.

All of us were ecstatic to be home after three months. I took my bag of dirty clothes and the suitcase home and left them next to the closet door. The suitcase remained untouched for a week.

Captain Salvatore said he was going to haul up the boat again at home, for we could hear a new rumbling sound on the stern of the boat. The *Ave Maria* was hauled and drydocked in Gloucester. I helped the boys haul up the boat and then I went home for lunch.

I opened the door and called, "Nina," only to be confronted by a wild tiger with fire and daggers in her eyes. She waved a lipstick-smeared handkerchief before me and screamed, "You bastard! Is this what you've been doing when you're away from home?"

I was innocent. I didn't even know what she was talking about. In a daze, I said, "Where did you get that handkerchief?"

"Where else but in your suitcase?" she answered. She burst into tears. "I'm going to show it to your mother and sister," she said.

Recalling the "Hi, big boy" incident, I tried to explain. It was no good.

"I trusted you" was all she said; she kept crying. I snatched the handkerchief out of her hand, ran down to the cellar, and burned it in the furnace.

Nina said, "You're guilty. You're burning the evidence."

"You're trying to make a big deal out of nothing," I hollered back. I kept trying to explain. She simply wouldn't listen. That night she slept with the children.

I found out we were going to be in port for ten days, and got a trenching site—a temporary job—aboard the dragger *Bonaventure*, captained by Joseph Novello. Meanwhile, Jerome Loiacano, our cook, a much older man than I but a very good friend, took a trenching site aboard the dragger *St. Christopher*, captained by Phil Filetto. The two boats left port together for the Liscome grounds north of Halifax, Nova Scotia.

We got our full trip of redfish in two days and immediately turned around for home. It would be a fifty-hour voyage. Somewhere on the way down, the two boats got separated in some fog.

When we got into port we heard the tragic news: the *St. Christopher* had been run down and sunk by an oil tanker. Two of her crew members were missing and presumed dead, including our cook and my friend, Jerome Loiacano.

When I arrived home, Nina hugged and kissed me, forgetting all her false ideas about me. This ended the only episode in my life that caused suspicion in my wife. Sometimes I would repeat the story to my friends and my wife would look at me, wink, and say, "Yeah, yeah, yeah."

By 1944, I was still aboard the *Ave Maria*. We had returned from the southern fisheries for the New England and Nova Scotian coasts. The demand for redfish was out of sight. The price was a stable seven cents a pound. Sometimes we could get a trip of 100,000 pounds in only one day. On those happy occasions, we'd come home days earlier than scheduled.

My stay on the *Ave Maria* ended when I had an argument with one of the crew members. I simply couldn't get along with this man. He was what we called a "grinder," always harping at someone. And I wasn't the type of guy to put up with this for long. Let's put it this way: in the interest of everyone aboard the boat, I got off. Otherwise, I think I would have killed him. Today, I am glad I made that decision.

The war was going well for the allies on all fronts. The government offered to give the boat *Jennie and Lucia* back to its original owners. Captain Joseph Brancaleone didn't want it back. He had built a ninety-foot dragger, the *Joseph and Lucia I.* Brancaleone's former partner, Lorenzo Susanno, took over the *Jennie and Lucia.*

Lorenzo was handicapped. He didn't know how to do the chartwork necessary to navigate the boat. He knew navigation only by memory. He approached me and asked if I'd come aboard to help him and his two sons, Leo and Joe, who were still very young. Lorenzo's two sons-in-law, my brothers Peter and Sammy, were in the Navy. I agreed to help him. I was the first mate and twinesman, for I had learned to build and mend nets with the best of them.

On this boat I met Johnny Ketchopoulos, the engineer running the 180 hp Cooper-Bessman direct-reversible engine below deck. Johnny and I became fast friends. All the men aboard were friendly. We all got along nicely. I was happy in my work, plotting courses and finding new fishing humps or hills on the ocean's floor. The redfish grouped together on these hills. Lorenzo allowed me to do everything a captain does. He treated me as a son, as we were almost family through the marriage of my brothers. At the close of 1944 and even into 1945, we alternated between groundfish and redfish. We'd go for whatever offered us the best price.

In December of 1944, I received a summons to report to Fort Banks in Winthrop for induction into the army. I left the Gloucester depot on a bus filled with other inductees. My heart was heavy, for I knew that, if I went, there was no telling what would happen to my wife, two small children, or my parents. My father couldn't go fishing and my mother was still very sick. As we rode toward Boston, I thought of all this. It seemed like a long one-hour drive.

Finally, we arrived and were separated like so many sheep. Those who had a grammar school education were sent to one side of the room and those who had high school or college educations went to the other.

We were hustled from doctor to doctor for the examination; I counted a total of twenty-three doctors. Then I told my hardship story to the psychiatrist. He just nodded his head and passed me along to the other doctors. Eventually, I was passed as physically fit and ordered to report to Camp Edwards on Cape Cod in ten days.

I couldn't believe it, the army! Not even the navy, after all the years I spent on boats and on the sea? I requested permission to see another psychiatrist and asked him to help me. If I was going into the service, at least put me in the navy, I demanded. My history showed I had been on the water all my life and I could be more useful in the navy, I said. His reply was "Why didn't you volunteer before they called you?" With that question, he dismissed me.

I went back to the bus filled with all the Gloucester men. Two pals suggested I come along to Boston for a "good-bye-to-civilian-life" blast in Scollay Square. "No thanks," I mumbled and climbed back on the bus, though I was quite capable of hoisting a few drinks with the best of them.

As I walked past Tony Parisi's barber shop in Gloucester, I was hailed by a familiar voice. "Hey, Salve. What's the matter? You look sad, Salve." It was Tony Parisi, who had cut my hair since my arrival here in Gloucester as a youngster. I told him my troubles. He said his good friend Leo Hennessey headed the draft board. "I'll call him and tell him your story," he said.

The next day, Tony told me to report to the draft board office on Main Street. "They'll review your case. Be there at two in the afternoon," he said.

I told the draft board that the government had taken three of my brothers for service in the navy, that I had a wife and two small children, that I supported my parents because my father was considered an enemy alien and couldn't go fishing and my mother was very sick and needed the attention of my father and that my other brother, Jimmy, was mentally and physically handicapped and required care. I stopped for breath. Now I was to go into the service. What would happen to my family?

The draft board told me to come back in a week. I replied that I didn't have a week, that I was ordered to report to Camp Edwards in the next few days. That night I couldn't sleep. All night I wondered what the decision would be. The draft board, meanwhile, checked on my story and started to untangle the mess. The board put me on "3-D status," meaning that I was deferred for three months after notifying army personnel. Three months later, I was given another three-month deferment.

Then came V-E Day—victory in Europe. The war was over in Europe. It was good fortune that I had come home from Fort Banks that day instead of going to Boston with my friends for a final drunken bash. Otherwise, I would have been a buck private in the occupation of Japan.

In August, we continued groundfishing on the *Jennie and Lucia*. We were taking out a trip in Boston one day when a call came through from Gloucester from my younger sister, Rosie. She said, "Hurry up to Salem Hospital, Salve. Mama's in critical condition."

I washed and dressed very quickly and hired a taxi to take me the seventeen miles to Salem. I was met at the hospital by my brother Peter, on leave from the navy, and my father, who was crying. Over and over, he repeated, "She's dead, she's dead."

With tears in my eyes, I walked into the room where my mother lay on a bed. A peaceful look rested on her face. I thought of all the worries and sacrifices she had made all her life, and I broke down and cried out loud. A young nurse, sobbing too, came over to comfort me. She had cared for Mama in her last days.

What a cruel blow Fate had dealt my mother! She had gotten sick just when the good times were about to arrive. She would never see all her sons come home safely from the war. On the horizon were better wages, improved living conditions and inventions of all kinds.

We had the wake in my mother's house on Mansfield Street because we weren't accustomed to funeral homes yet. The wake lasted three days. We got word through the Red Cross that my brother Tony was on his way home from the Pacific. His travel arrangements got fouled up and he didn't arrive until weeks later. We couldn't trace Sammy, who was also in the Pacific with the invasion forces.

In the meantime, I gave orders to James Greely, the mortician, to hold my mother's body in a cool vault and wait for my brother. When Tony finally got home, my father, Peter, Lawrence and I opened the coffin again. Sammy never got a chance to see his mother again. After we all paid our respects, she was buried in the family plot I had bought at Calvary Cemetery.

That summer, while in port, we heard the news that a powerful new bomb, the atomic bomb, had exploded in Hiroshima, Japan. The air force had dropped it, killing and wounding tens of thousands of people. A new age of science—and warfare—had begun.

On the *Jennie and Lucia*, we had switched over from dragging to go seining for mackerel. We went south to Block Island to fish for mackerel that fetched nine cents a pound. We could sometimes catch a trip in one or two days, far preferable to the one-week trips we took for dragging. We came in on August 9 with 70,000 pounds of mackerel and heard the jarring news that a second, more powerful bomb had been dropped on Nagasaki. The Japanese government was going to make an unconditional surrender. The war would be over soon. For a few days, the talk of surrender continued. I hoped that all my brothers would be spared and come home safely.

My family was worried about Sammy. We hadn't heard a word from him for months. We didn't realize the reason for the silence. General Douglas MacArthur was preparing to invade Japan, and Sammy was part of it. After the bomb was used, all plans for the invasion were called off, sparing thousands of American casualties.

We landed two more trips of mackerel before hearing the news of the Japanese surrender while in New Bedford. The surrender came at 7 A.M., August 24. All fighting ceased. If ever there was a cause to celebrate, victory in Japan—V-J Day—was it. Four crew members and I took a walk into downtown. People were tremendously excited. I could feel an electricity; a wild night was beginning. When we passed a liquor store, the owner was boarding up his plate-glass windows. He had sensed trouble too.

We each bought a quart of whiskey, took big slugs, and joined the crowd of celebrants. Everyone was kissing and hugging. The war, which had changed the lives of millions of people all over the world, was finally over. We were all in the same boat, toasting our new happiness and joy, and trying to forget, at least for the night, all the destruction.

Around midnight, with the crowds still as wild as ever and the five of us feeling good, our mate Frank Muise passed out on the street. I picked up Frank, who weighed 200 pounds, and threw him on my shoulders. "We can't leave him lying in the street," I grunted.

With John Ketchopoulos and Leo Ciaramitaro in tow, we headed for the wharf. With Frank still resting on my shoulders, I did a foolish thing, or so the crew later told me. I held Frank in my arms, the way you hold a baby, and jumped six feet down to the deck, landing upright with Frank still in my arms. He was unconscious. If I had slipped, the two of us would have been the latest casualties in the celebration of the war's end.

I slid him down the fo'c'sle ladder and dumped him on top of a bunk. Then I said to Johnny and Leo, "Let's go back to the street and party some more." Leo and Johnny had bewildered looks on their faces. They couldn't believe it. It took superhuman strength to get Frank Muise to bed like that, they said, but I said it was only the whiskey.

By four in the morning, we had had enough and came aboard for some sleep. Around six, I felt a hand shaking me awake. It was Lorenzo, who had decided to go home to Gloucester while I was trying to sleep it off. We were already outside New Bedford Harbor but had run into fog. Now Lorenzo had awakened me for a compass course to the Cape Cod Canal.

I plotted a course on the chart, gave him a reading, and passed out again. Luckily, I hit the right course. Otherwise, we would never have made it to the canal. I don't remember any of this. The captain and crew told me about it later.

HONEYMOONERS

Everyone needed a vacation at the end of the war. I got my chance to get away from Gloucester when the lumpers and fish cutters voted a strike. They wanted more money. The whole waterfront shut down, which meant the whole city shut down. The fish processors passed the word to the boats that we might as well stay in port, because nobody would buy a catch of fish until that strike was settled. The processors controlled the fleet. Hell, the fish could rot on our decks before the processors would let an outsider come in and buy it.

A bust at the cutting houses on the waterfront meant a boon for the boat repair yards. Most of the skippers had their boats put up on the marine railways and hauled out of the harbor for scraping and painting.

My pal Johnny Ketchopoulos came up with the bright idea of taking the wives on vacation. I agreed immediately. The death of my mother, all the responsibilities during the war years—I wanted to forget and get away. I hadn't been off Cape Ann more than five times during the war unless I was at sea.

"Nina, let's go on a honeymoon," I said. "I haven't taken you any-place since the day we were married. That was only a trip to Boston. What do you say?" Nina needed little persuading.

My brother Peter, and his wife, Jenny, were friends of the Ketchopoulos family too and jumped at the chance to come along. Peter had taken over as skipper of the *Jennie and Lucia*, his father-in-law's boat, and had three children, Rosemary, Virginia and Peter, Jr. All three were beautiful, blond babies and kept Peter and Jenny going around the clock.

Johnny Ketchopoulos and his wife, Shirley, picked up the gang in a 1941 DeSoto four-door sedan, one of the last cars made before the factories swung into war production. Johnny, Peter and I pooled $500 and took turns picking up the tab during the ten-day trip.

Johnny did the driving and I "navigated," the road map open on my lap. We set out a course for the Old Man of the Mountains in Franconia Notch, New Hampshire. After sightseeing and taking pictures, we then moved on to Vermont and across the border.

We found Montreal to be a lovely city. We spent three days there, visiting churches, museums and nightclubs, taking pictures, and buying toys for the children. At an Indian village tourist attraction, Nina and I bought war drums, bows and arrows, headgear, and toy tomahawks for the boys. I picked out a pair of beaded baby moccasins for the little girl we hoped to have someday. I'd have to wait for grandchildren before having a little girl in the family.

We reentered the United States near Rochester, New York, and traveled west to the famous honeymoon resort, Niagara Falls. Everyone had the same idea. We couldn't find rooms and finally settled for a run-down place outside the city. The next day we took a close look at the falls from the *Maid of the Mist* passenger boat. We took photographs and stood in awe of Mother Nature.

We landed in New York City. We had rooms in the heart of Times Square and spent the days sightseeing and evenings nightclubbing. Johnny and Peter loved to have a few cocktails and would often end up feeling jolly. I limited myself to a drink or two, trying to stay alert. After all, we were strangers in a strange place.

Soon enough, we were almost broke. Johnny and Peter wanted one more night out on the town. I wanted to see the Broadway play, *Oklahoma!* I put my hand in a secret pocket and pulled out three crisp hundred-dollar bills. I loaned them each one, saying, "You go back to your nightclub, but I'm going to the playhouse." I always carried extra money. I always thought about the future. It was part of being the oldest son in a poor family. Nina and I greatly enjoyed *Oklahoma!* We shopped at Macy's department store the next day and then returned home.

It was a delightful trip for Nina and me. Our next vacation came twenty-three years later.

JOHNNY BABY

After the war, my brothers Peter and Sammy joined their father-in-law, Lorenzo Susanno, aboard the *Jennie and Lucia*. I got a site aboard the *Frances R.*, which was captained by Bill Ragusa. His brother Charlie and I worked on deck together, and I doubled as the cook after the regular cook quit.

I was anxious to work for myself. I was convinced that unless I got my own boat, I would never get ahead and, more important, get to spend any time with my family. In the summer of 1946, I found my boat, a 46-foot dragger named *Sylvia M.* My brother Tony and I went into partnership and bought the boat which I rechristened the *Johnny Baby* after my first son. My recollection is that the boat cost $6,500, most of which was my money. We rigged for dragging and made as many improvements to the engine as we could afford, but try as we did, the engine kept balking and cost us much time, aggravation and money during our first two trips. We finally quit on it and put in a new compact 110 hp General Motors engine. The engine alone cost almost as much as the whole boat had cost us and it would be years before we caught up.

I was Captain and my father joined Tony on deck. We concentrated on whiting, bringing them in "H and G'ed"—without head or guts. That meant a lot of deckwork for four cents a pound. At least the two-month absences from home were a thing of the past.

Soon we realized we had serious trouble on our hands. We were taking on water every trip. Leaks opened up when the nails popped loose from the planks. The *Johnny Baby* was hauled out of the water and the leaks filled. The workmen told us the boat's sorry history. The *Sylvia M.* had been built with common house nails. Salt water rusted the nails and caused leaks. I went further in the hole putting galvanized nails into the boat.

Tony wanted out. Why not? We were paying out money a hundred times faster than we were taking it in. "Salve, sell the boat," Tony said. "I'm going fishing on the big boats and make some money." I was offered $7,000 for the boat. I refused to sell. Seven thousand dollars didn't do much against debts of $13,000. I owed the banks, the marine railways, and the ship chandlers for nets and supplies.

God, I was stubborn. "I'll take over everything," I told Tony. "Let me pay off the other debts first, then I'll square the fifteen hundred you put up with you."

Tony went fishing on the big boats and my father and I continued to slog it out on the *Johnny Baby*. I had to hire fifteen- or sixteen-year-old boys to crew the boat because all the grown men worked the big boats for the big money. I was a tough skipper, but I think I was a fair one. Many rewards came later in life, including the respect of these young men. Some of these youngsters became top-notch captains and later reminded me of my hot temper aboard the *Johnny Baby*.

I lost my temper when I was under a lot of pressure. Sometimes there were no teenagers to take out on the boat. Sometimes my father couldn't fish. Winter came, and there was no money coming in at all. The bills kept coming. I was afraid of losing the house on Mansfield Street. My father lived alone now downstairs and Nina and I and the boys lived upstairs. The monthly mortgage payment was less than $100, but I couldn't pay it and still take care of the boat repair, insurance and supply bills.

My mother-in-law loaned Nina and me $300 to see us through the winter of 1947. I repaid the loan in a couple of months, but the struggle to get out of debt lasted for many years. Nina stood by me and never doubted my dream of having my own boys on deck with me.

During one especially gloomy period, I was forced to tie up the *Johnny Baby* and take a site aboard an offshore dragger, the *St. Joseph*, captained by Jerome Lovasco. I split my earnings from the *St. Joseph* between household bills and debts against the *Johnny Baby*. I hated to steam past the tied-up boat from the deck of another boat. I felt I had failed. Yet fishing was the only thing I knew how to do and, by God, I'd keep fishing to make something of myself and provide for my family.

One summer I tried to fish alone. My father was too old now and all the youngsters were on the big boats. Doing the job alone was impossible. The *Johnny Baby* had a shallow keel, causing it to drift when the wheel was left unattended. I couldn't steer the boat and do the deckwork. Setting out the net was complicated business. The net and the other trawlboard, the "doors" that kept the net spread open on the ocean's floor, had to be handled precisely.

I tried tying a rope becket to the wheel to keep the *Johnny Baby* steady while I worked on deck. But that failed, too. The drag of the doors would pull the bow of the boat to the starboard side, then the boards would flip over and snarl on the main cables. It caused me great anguish and I raged out loud. I'd bang my head against the mast in frustration and look up at the sky, shaking my fist and saying, "I'm tougher than you are. I'm not going to give up and quit."

I was sure I couldn't fish the *Johnny Baby* alone. I needed help with the cables and the nets. Nina always had words of gentle encouragement. "Tomorrow is another day, Salve," she'd say. "Probably you'll find someone to go out with tomorrow."

I shook my head, almost ready to admit defeat. One night I couldn't sleep because of my worrying. How was I going to support my family? Would we be as poor as I was as a kid? The questions haunted me. That morning, I woke up Johnny and told Nina I was taking him fishing. Johnny was only seven years old, but I desperately needed him. It was just as my father desperately needed me many years earlier.

When we got to the fishing grounds, I told Johnny he was captain. I put him behind the wheel. He listened carefully as I instructed him on steering to the port side as I released the brake drums and let out the wire and doors. We gave it a try. Johnny kept the wheel turned just enough to let the net slip into the water. Success at last!

When we hauled back, I put Johnny to work on the hoister, a dangerous job. With the use of a rope and a block and tackle, Johnny swung the bag of fish out of the ocean and onto the deck. We called it the "cod-end." Aboard the *Johnny Baby*, the cod-end contained as much as 3,000 pounds of fish, usually whiting. "Be careful and just dip the rope if it snarls," I told Johnny.

Johnny managed to get two baskets down safely before dropping one on my head. The poor kid was tired. He didn't have the strength to handle the job yet. I slipped a line between the basket handles and lowered them down to the fish hold one by one. When I had six baskets in the hold, I'd jump down, dump the fish in wooden boxes, even off the ice and nail the covers tight. Meanwhile, Johnny continued filling the baskets up on deck.

The system worked. All summer long we worked together. I was very proud of my partner. We'd come into Gloucester Harbor with forty to sixty boxes of whiting—5,000 to 7,500 pounds of fish—when our luck held out. Our dealer paid $2.50 per box. We were making good money again. We cleared $100 or $150 a day after paying fuel, ice and food bills. Our profits were limited only by the weather, for I wouldn't take any chances on sloppy weather with my seven-year-old son aboard.

We had some hard days, too . . . days of setting the net out and hauling it back empty. All day long we set and hauled back, finally coming to the same sorry conclusion: there were no fish around. I gained a lot of useful information and experience in those days.

Thus, the struggle continued. I'd pay my bills and climb two-thirds up the ladder of success, only to come tumbling down again with boat troubles or a spell of poor luck finding fish. I climbed right back up again and took my chances at being knocked off again.

TROUBLE ON THE *DARTMOUTH*

In my desperation to get ahead, I once accepted a trenching site that I soon regretted. We had finally hauled the *Johnny Baby* out of the water at Alex Chisholm's Rocky Neck Marine Railways to correct the shallow keel. The drydock manager said the problem could be corrected by deepening the underhull keel by a foot, at a price of $800.

Even when I wasn't fishing, I always woke up before dawn. While the *Johnny Baby* was on the rails, I was on the wharf anxiously inspecting the hull work by sunup. One morning my brother Sammy and I walked across the causeway to the Rocky Bay Fish Company and nearby foodshop for a sandwich and drink. The dragger *Dartmouth* was taking out fish there. On deck, I spotted my friend Johnny Ketchopoulos, the engineer, and hailed him. "Did you have a good trip?" I asked.

"Ah, so-so," he said. Johnny explained that they would have had a much better trip but were constantly tearing up the net. The *Dartmouth* men didn't know much about mending and were about to rig a new net. I looked closely at the net.

"The twine's all here," I said. "All you have to do is fit it right. You don't need to change nets." I took a needle and twine and started at the bottom wing section. I put another crew member to work mending the bottom belly. Soon I had two others work across the top square. Four of us did the job in two hours' time.

When the captain came aboard, I recognized him as Mac, who had been the engineer on the boat *Ave Maria* a few years back. "I didn't know you were captain," I said, remembering him as the engineer who always slept in the relatively comfortable fo'c'sle, instead of the engine room where he belonged. Once we had hung up the net on a sunken wreck, and by the time he got to the engine room to throw the clutch, we'd lost the net and some wire cable.

I knew Mac, all right. And I didn't particularly like him, either. Still, I was willing to give a guy a chance to prove himself.

"Yeah, I'm captain," he said and introduced the owner. Mac asked what I was doing, and when I said I was in for ten days because of repairs to my boat, he asked me to make a trenching trip with him. He said I would be the first mate. "There's twenty-five dollars for you at the end of the trip, and the owner will throw in another twenty-five," he said. That meant fifty dollars over and above my share. I quickly agreed. Hell, I needed the money.

"How about taking Sammy along, too; he knows how to mend real good," I said. Mac agreed to that, too. Sammy and I split the thirty dollars the owner gave me for repairing the net. We left Rocky Neck gladdened by the sudden turn of events.

Two days later, Sammy and I showed up at the *Dartmouth* at dawn to begin the trip. The harbor was obscured in a thick fog. We went aboard and introduced ourselves to the crew. I knew most of the crew, including two of Mac's brothers-in-law and a colored man called "Sweet Pea."

Sweet Pea was a good worker when he felt like it. Apparently, he had gained a sense of freedom in New England, compared to the southern fisheries. Sweet Pea was a happy-go-lucky, laughing type and kept us in stitches all the time.

The 90-foot *Dartmouth* had four sister boats: the *Benny and Josephine*, the *Philip and Grace*, the *Baby Rose* and the *St. Victoria*. The *Dartmouth* was double-rigged with a gallast on both sides, meaning she could work the nets on either the starboard or port side, a great advantage. She also had a 180 hp Cooper-Bessman engine and could do ten miles per hour. She was an able and good seaboat.

At 9 A.M., the fog lifted and we cast off lines to get under way. Suddenly, the fog closed in again. Captain Mac was quite upset. He hadn't run into fog during his three-trip command. He halted the *Dartmouth* so we could listen for the fog bell on Ten Pound Island, then panicked and wanted to turn back to the wharf again. The captain on the dragger *Dolphin* radioed that all was clear outside the breakwater. After a lot of persuasion from the crew, Mac agreed to push on and we finally got out of the harbor. I was thinking, *This guy knows nothing. He doesn't even trust himself.* I figured I had made a big mistake.

Mac called his pal on the *Dolphin* and had him slow down. We caught the *Dolphin* and together proceeded for Cape Cod. We caught 10,000 pounds of mixed fish in two days before a strong northwest gale forced us to Provincetown Harbor for shelter. When the winds died out, we headed in a southerly direction to Georges Bank, staying close to the *Dolphin*. We dragged twenty to twenty-two fathoms of water, catching an average of 1,000 pounds of haddock per tow. A fleet of Boston beam trawlers kept us company. After two days of this, a breeze freshened from the southeast. Weather reports said a fast-moving storm was coming, with plenty of rain and winds up to fifty miles per hour. By nightfall, the winds already were over thirty miles per hour.

Looking about I noticed all the lights from the Boston beam trawlers fading to the south-southeast. It was getting very sloppy on deck and the winds howled like banshees through the rigging and otter trawl boards on deck.

As our last tow produced only 300 pounds of haddock, Captain Mac ordered us to leave the net and otter trawlboards on deck. "We're going to lay to and jog it out," he said, ordering the crew to rig a "riding sail" between the two spars so we could drift with the storm.

Johnny Ketchopoulos shut down the engines and we laid to. I went to the fo'c'sle to have coffee and a sandwich. "What are we going to do?" asked the cook. "What Captain Mac says, lay to and jog," I said. Neither the cook nor I was convinced Mac was doing the right thing.

Meanwhile, some of the boys got into the bunks. I went on deck, holding the lifeline rigged between the two masts to keep myself from being blown off the deck. Rain and ocean spray flew all over the deck. The ocean looked like a pot of boiling water. Sammy was on watch in the pilothouse. "It's going to be a nasty night, Salve," he said. I agreed.

The captain and engineer were down below in their bunks. I snapped on a light over the chart table and began studying the charts. I switched on the radio direction finder, pulled the headset over my ears and listened for signals from Coast Guard stations on Cape Cod and from the Nantucket Lightship. I plotted straight lines from the signals and fixed our position.

To my horror, we were only fifteen miles east of a large area of shoal water, only five to ten fathoms deep, and in some places even more shallow. I checked my bearing again. And again, the same. I went below for the captain. I told him about the shoal water.

"Don't worry," he said.

"With a southeast gale blowing, Mac, we'll drift on those shoals and there's no telling what will happen. We could be shipwrecked. Besides," I questioned him, "what happened to the Boston fishing fleet that was with us?"

"I don't know."

"You don't know?" Instantly, I felt the same old intense dislike for this man. The captain was supposed to look out for his crew. Mac couldn't have cared less. "Every one of those boats has steamed south-southeast, going into the wind to get into deep water," I said, trying my best to hold back my rage. "The ocean's sixty fathoms deep only thirty miles from here. I'll bet that's where they went."

"Don't bother me," he said. And with that, Mac shut his eyes and went back to sleep. I couldn't believe it. Back in the fo'c'sle I woke the crew and related the conversation, telling them to back me up in case of trouble. "If we don't steam away we'll be lost on the shoals," I said.

The crew assured me that they'd back up my decision to steam for the deep water. I returned to find Mac sleeping. I woke up John Ketchopoulos and told him to start the engines. As the engines roared, Mac woke up and said, "So now you're the captain." I ignored him and went to the pilothouse and rang the bell to go ahead. Sammy held the wheel on a south-southeasterly course.

The *Dartmouth* took the seas beautifully. There was no hard pounding. In three hours, we dropped over the bank into the deep water and came upon the Boston and New Bedford beam trawler fleet lying into the wind. The crew sighed with relief when they saw all the other boats. Sweet Pea nicknamed Captain Mac "Captain Mistake." I had lost all confidence in him.

After thirty-four hours, the storm died. The next day we fished, scratching away at 700 pounds of haddock per tow. On the second day I was on deck when Mac called me to the wheelhouse. He was all excited.

"The radio telephone is squawking in Italian," he said. "What are they saying?"

I recognized the voices. Joe Ciaramitaro, captain of the *Benjamin C.*, and Snake Nicastro, captain of the *Felicia*, were trading information. Joe said he needed only one more set to top off the pens and head for Gloucester. I cut in and asked Snake, in Italian, where they were fishing.

"Salve, what boat are you on?"

"The *Dartmouth*."

"What's your position?"

I gave him the position and he plotted a course. "Run an hour and a half on this course and you'll be on us," he assured me. "There's plenty of fish," he added in Italian.

The *Benjamin C.* and *Felicia* steamed away with holds full of haddock just as we arrived in the *Dartmouth.* We set out and in two hours had 8,000 pounds of haddock. I was on deck, gutting, cutting and washing with the rest of the crew. We were a happy bunch now that we were on fish. All night we kept busy. Mac and I alternated time at the wheel. By the end of the next day we had picked up 65,000 pounds of haddock.

We decided to run to Gloucester while the prices were still high. The *Benjamin C.* and *Felicia* got fourteen cents per pound. Two days later, we got eleven cents—still a good price. Each man got a gross share of $700.

When I think of Captain Mac I shake my head in disbelief. His uncle was a top-notch captain, a highliner, getting the best commands of the fleet. Mac didn't have it. He loved to sleep too much. A good captain sleeps with one eye open. Poor judgment can lead to disaster.

I split my $700 between the railways and support for my family. The deep keel worked out fine.

THE FISHERMAN'S WHARF

In the late spring of 1950, twenty-three captains and small boat owners held a meeting in an empty warehouse on the waterfront. The meeting was called because we were fed up with being pushed around from wharf to wharf by the fish processors, who owned and controlled the docks.

The solution was to buy our own wharf. And for $23,000 we could buy the old Ben Pine wharf, which had been gutted by a recent fire. The pilings were sound.

That's how the Fisherman's Wharf Corporation was born. Each of us pledged $1,000 for ten shares. Immediately we were berthing our boats at the wharf and shipping our catches to the New York markets. Soon we were also selling fuel oil, boxes, and other supplies to pay our expenses.

On the day I pledged my $1,000 I didn't have a dime to my name. In fact, I was deeply in debt. I couldn't pass up this chance and decided to go to a local bank for a loan. The vice president shuffled me off to the head man. When I asked for the thousand, this Mr. Big asked why I needed the money, suspecting that I might be in on this new cooperative wharf. I told him I had to haul out the boat and build an expensive new net.

The bigwigs in town, the fish processors and their backers, were afraid of the competition we represented on the wharf. Before the co-op, fishermen sold all their catches locally and were at the mercy of the processors. Now we were independent. If we felt like selling in Gloucester, we did. If not, we'd ship to New York.

After years of struggling to band together and almost breaking apart several times, today we are well established and strong. The building and piers are repaired and modernized.

Fisherman's Wharf is now worth many times the original $23,000-investment. None of the original boats are left today, and of the twenty-three captains that started the corporation, seven have died and left their shares to their sons. Some have retired, as I did in 1983.

The years went by, and I went on fishing with many different crews. One winter day in the early fifties I took *Johnny Baby* five miles south of Gloucester on a calm but very cold day. The temperature was thirteen degrees below zero. Paul DeMaria, and my *compare*, Joe Loiacano, old shipmates aboard the *Rose and Lucy*, had decided to come out and fish with me.

As we set out, the boards and cable wires became tangled. I came out of the pilothouse without a hat and worked the wires. After fifteen minutes, I was back in the pilothouse, which was heated by a portable kerosene stove. My right ear tingled. When I touched it, my ear felt hard and smooth, like a little piece of glass.

Joe said the ear was white. I put the palm of my hand over the ear and held it there, because I had heard stories that fingers and ears snap off after they've been frostbitten. "Let's haul back and head for home so a doctor can look at that," Joe said.

I shook my head, no. I dipped my handkerchief in a bucket of seawater—all the fresh water aboard was frozen solid—and placed it against my ear for five minutes. I felt pain and a burning sensation. The blood was circulating again.

We set out and hauled back three times and caught 2,000 pounds of flounder, mostly black backs and some yellowtail dabs. At six cents a pound, we fetched about $120 for the trip, or twenty-five dollars per man after expenses.

I almost lost my ear for that twenty-five dollars. In fact, the money went to a doctor who examined the ear. He wrapped it in bandages, making me look like a Turk. It took more than a week for the ear to heal. First, it swelled to nearly twice its normal size and turned black and then it peeled. I went fishing anyway. When the bandages came off, I took to wearing a stocking cap in the winter.

THE *LINDA B.*

Nina gave birth to our third son, Joseph, in March of 1950. According to Sicilian tradition, March is St. Joseph's month, and so we chose that name for our newborn. Nina wanted to name the baby for me. I resisted. "You don't have any sons named after you yet," she said.

"My sons can name their children after me," I said. Sicilian tradition was to name the firstborn son after his grandfather and to carry on the Christian names on an every-other-generation basis. My father was named for his grandfather; I was named after my grandfather; my firstborn was named for his grandfather.

I still had bad memories of the kids calling me "Rosie" in the schoolyard and didn't want to put my son through the same thing. I had gotten into a lot of fights because of the name Rosario. Later, I insisted on being called "Salve," short for my middle name, Salvatore.

With three young children and a wife to support, I really had to hustle. My approach to fishing was very aggressive, often taking the *Johnny Baby* out in questionable weather. I always managed to find places to work in the lee of the land—the areas protected from high winds by land masses.

My gambling ways paid off nicely in the early fifties; my family lived much better than my brothers and I had as children. I have to admit that I secretly enjoyed the occasional risks involved in taking the boat out in high seas.

In April of 1953, however, my aggressive approach cost me the *Johnny Baby*. Luckily, my two-member crew and I survived. We had decided to go out despite ample warning. The winds from the southwest had blown thirty miles an hour the night before. When Lawrence, Billy LaFond, and I arrived at the wharf at dawn, the winds had almost died out. Still, the seas ran five or six feet as we rounded Eastern Point, the *Johnny Baby* pounding hard as we bucked into the sea.

There was no wind to worry about, and that gave me a false sense of security. When we reached the fishing grounds six miles off Eastern Point, I noticed another boat just due west of us, near Halfway Rock. I felt even more assured.

The reason both of us were out in this sloppy weather, of course, was greed. We were counting on a high flounder price while most of the fleet stayed tied up in port.

As the boat lurched and rolled with the seas, Lawrence, Billy, and I set out the net. Half an hour later, I routinely lifted the trapdoor out of the pilothouse floor to inspect the engine room. I was stunned by what I saw.

Floorboards, oilcans and bags of rags floated in two feet of water. Water was spraying everywhere. At least the engine was running. I hollered to the crew in the fo'c'sle, where they had gone to sleep in bunks as we dragged.

"Get those handpumps working," I shouted, then grabbed the radio to send the Coast Guard a distress message. I turned the *Johnny Baby* in the direction of the boat we had spotted earlier. The 52-foot shrimp dragger *St. John*, which was our only hope, stood four miles west of us. With our net over the side, it would take us forty minutes to get to it.

"Sam, we're taking on water fast," I radioed to the *St. John*'s captain, Salvatore Nicastro. "Come for us."

Sam had already hauled back his net and begun steaming at peak speed toward us. I ordered the crew to unfasten the ten-foot skiff which was tied to the top of the pilothouse. Just then, we took a huge wave broadside. The *Johnny Baby* rolled with it as water poured into the fish hold. I couldn't risk our lives any longer. "Abandon the boat," I ordered.

The *Johnny Baby* threatened to roll over at any second, trapping the three of us underwater in the pilothouse. We leaped into the skiff and Lawrence furiously rowed us away from the lurching, sinking boat. Just seconds before the bow disappeared beneath the water, we heard a muffled explosion. The air trapped in the forward compartment was releasing itself, ripping apart the *Johnny Baby*'s bow.

Gulp. She was gone.

The *St. John* was still a mile away when the *Johnny Baby* disappeared, stern-first. Lawrence, Billy, and I huddled speechless as the big seas bobbed our punt skiff up and down like a little rubber ball. We felt so small in that big expanse of ocean. Lawrence kept the skiff turned into the rolling seas, as we were afraid of being swamped. Only a few inches of freeboard showed on the skiff's sides.

I thought about how helpless we were. It occurred to me that I couldn't swim well; not that it mattered much out there. In fact, most fishermen couldn't swim. Everything happened so fast, we had even left the life preservers behind.

The *St. John* finally came alongside us and we scrambled aboard. A Coast Guard 44-footer arrived minutes later, expecting to tow us to port, but only an oil slick and some floating debris remained of the *Johnny Baby*.

The Coast Guard ferried the three of us to port, allowing the *St. John* to go back to fishing. At the station, someone handed me a cup of coffee. I was wet and cold, trembling and dazed with fright. I was overwhelmed at losing my life's work in that boat. What could I show for years of struggle? I had only about $8,000 in insurance money, half of which would go to paying off the bank loan.

Seven years of work was gone in less than half an hour. My mind filled with painful memories: my first sight of the *Johnny Baby*, the struggles to fish her along, young Johnny at the wheel, the overhauls, the new engine, the new keel. All gone. All I'd get was a lousy four grand.

Two days later, I was fishing in the big boats. To hell with the memories. There was no unemployment compensation. There were no relief payments. I had to support my family, and fishing was the only trade I knew. Naturally, I hustled around the waterfront.

I worked all summer on one big boat after another. By September, I was scouting around for a new boat. Of course, Nina was against the idea, at least at first. "Don't you think we've been through enough? The sacrifices, the going without, while all the money gets spent on the boat?" she demanded.

"I don't care, Nina," I said, my old stubborn self. " I want another boat." Then Nina shocked me. She produced $1,000 in war bonds. I had no idea she had any savings at all. "Here," she said, handing over the bonds with a little smile. "Go get yourself a boat."

That ended Nina's dream of buying a new house, for she wanted to move out of the crowded Mansfield Street neighborhood. She did finally get her house—thirty-four years later.

In late August of 1955, I bought a new boat, the *Linda B.*, for $14,500 from John Bennett, Jr. Sammy Ciaramitaro, of the Gloucester Grocery, helped me secure a bank loan of $10,000. I met Bennett through Ray Kershaw, manager of the Whiting Association at Fisherman's Wharf. Bennett was a marine welder. He and his father, a high school chemistry teacher in Quincy, had spent three years building the *Linda B.* in their backyard. They took great pride in their work.

Young Bennett had tried to make a living at fishing, but he couldn't make a go of it. He simply wasn't an experienced fisherman and had to hire a captain while he worked as crew. Since he had to pay the skipper a high percentage of the gross, there just wasn't enough left over for him after expenses.

When I bought the *Linda B.*, she was seven years old and very sturdy. In fact, she's still doing the job today. She was powered by a 165 hp Walkershaw diesel engine, and swung a forty-inch propeller. She could make almost ten miles an hour.

When I agreed to buy *Linda B.*, I immediately had her moved from Rose's Wharf to Fisherman's Wharf. I was wary of the boat's gear being stripped, not by Bennett, but by people who literally made a living out of stripping boats after they had been sold and before the new owner could get them fishing. This was, unfortunately, a common practice when boats were sold; it could cost the new owner thousands of dollars. You had to have both eyes open on the waterfront.

Don Hunter, the engineer who had worked on the *Linda B.* for Bennett, helped me bring her to Fisherman's Wharf. "What are you going to do now?" I asked him.

"I guess I have to look for another site," he answered.

"How'd you like to come fishing with me?" I asked. His experience with the engine would be a tremendous help to me. Don agreed. We ended up fishing together for seven years. He was a hard worker and really knew his engines. I often gave him a cash bonus because of the respect I felt for him. Most of us in the fishing business were related by blood or marriage, and those that weren't had to earn our respect and create the necessary trust.

Hunter, Nino Parisi, my brother-in-law Tony DaCruz, and I became the crew of the *Linda B.* Even before shoving off from the dock, Don stuck his head out of the engine room and said, "Salve, we have big troubles. I found water in the oil-slick pan." That meant major problems, either a cracked cylinder head or a cracked manifold.

"Oh no," I groaned, "not again." Was history repeating itself? I wondered. I'm starting off with a new boat with all kinds of troubles again. I called John Bennett and told him of the troubles. "I haven't even gone out from the dock yet," I said. "I paid good money for the boat and you're responsible for the troubles."

To my surprise, Bennett said, "I'll take care of it." And he did. He sent a mechanic to Gloucester for two weeks to do a complete overhaul—new pistons, new manifold, new bearings, everything. Parts and labor cost over $2,500. Bennett paid for it all and even paid Don something for helping in the repair job. I have to admit John Bennett was a good man in helping pay all the cost in repairing the engine. I was broke now, after investing everything in the *Linda B.* To this day, John still works on our three family boats, and my sons and I have nothing but respect for his work and his integrity.

When we finally got the *Linda B.* beyond the breakwater, I felt a tremendous difference between this boat and the *Johnny Baby.* We had all the power we'd need and she was a terrific sea boat, able to take the kind of beating that broke the *Johnny Baby.*

Now I could compete with the bigger boats at Fisherman's Wharf. God, I was so ambitious, so happy. I'd rub my hands together with delight just thinking about the future. The first week alone we shared up at $300 a man. Everyone was happy and just as full of ambition as I was. It was a good omen. Right from the beginning, we were making good money on this new, wonderful boat.

Our pace was slowed only by the winter weather. High winds and freezing temperatures would keep the whole fleet in port. Still, most days I found places in the lee of the land to fish.

Now I could put all my experience to good use. I had tremendous trust in the *Linda B.* and sometimes took her as far north as Monhegan, Maine. There we'd fish greysoles and dabs, which got good prices compared to the whiting. Steadily, slowly, I started to pay off the boat and again provide a decent living for my family.

In November of 1955, Nina gave birth to our fourth son, Thomas. He was named after her brother, the same Tommy ("Tom Brady") Randazza who had urged his mother to grab me for marriage to Nina. I was delighted with the name, for Tommy was always a special friend to me.

Meanwhile, my oldest son, Johnny, had quit high school during his freshman year. He had started the year but secretly had been skipping school. His counselor arranged a meeting with Nina and me and told us Johnny wanted to go fishing. The counselor, surprisingly enough, advised me to take him fishing. "If he gets sick of it after a year, he can always come back to school."

He never went back to school. Johnny was a big help to me. He was the one crew member I could count on as the others came and went. Of course, it worked both ways. Johnny learned a lot of valuable mechanics from Don Hunter and Tony DaCruz. Tony had married my sister Rose.

My father still came fishing with us occasionally. I took him aboard only during the fair-weather weeks of summer. He cooked for us and did some light work, as he was seventy two years old. The fresh air and activity were good for his health. He enjoyed the company and would tell Johnny stories of trawling for fish out of Boston and the traditions of the old country which he had left so many years ago. Dad spoke Sicilian, and Johnny picked up the language. He's the only one of my four sons who speaks it.

My father lived until he was eighty-six. When he died in 1968, it was cancer that took him. He spent the last couple of years in a nursing home, but I would visit him there every time I came in from a trip. I avoided seeing him during the final days, though, because the sight of this strong, rugged man wasting away to less than ninety pounds broke my heart. It was selfish not to go in the last days, but I think he understood. His mind was alert right to the end.

The fifties were so exciting for me. My sons were helping to work the whole family out of debt and into prosperity. Salvatore would fish with us when he wasn't in school, and Joey, by the time he was seven, would be with us on deck, too. My boys learned to work as a real crew during the school vacations. I paid them according to what they did, starting at a quarter share, and letting them work their way up, as I did. Nina would buy their clothes and save the rest of their earnings in a bank account. Each would receive a little nest egg when he married.

In late July of 1958, we suffered another setback. The engine block cracked and it would cost $6,500 to have it replaced. There was no way I could pay that kind of money. I shopped around in New Bedford at Hathaway Machine Company with Ray Kershaw, who had connections in Gloucester's rival port, and talked to Lenny Motta, the engine agent.

We found a whole new Walkershaw 195 hp engine for $8,500, plus $3,000 more for installation. I figured, why pay over $6,000 for an engine block when I can get a whole new engine for $5,000 more? The catch on the new engine was that we had to have it installed in New Bedford.

I put a second mortgage on the *Linda B.* and went ahead with plans for the new engine. My sons were all growing up now, so I figured I'd have plenty of help doing most of the installation work myself. My wife wasn't so convinced. "Here we go again, Salve," she said. "We're starting all over again."

I assured her that the boys and I could do the job. I was still a young man and very ambitious. The biggest problem we had was getting the boat, cracked engine block and all, to New Bedford. We were willing to have another fishing boat tow us there, but the government wasn't so willing. Only a licensed tugboat was permitted to tow through the Cape Cod Canal. That would cost $2,000. I made up my mind to get the *Linda B.* there myself.

We poured a sealing solution into the engine and started it. As long as the engine was running, the pressure would hold water in the block. Johnny, Salvatore, Joey and Tommy all made the trip with me. We left Gloucester at midnight and arrived at the Cape Cod Canal at dawn. We got through the canal without a problem, but found a thick fog bank on the western side, forcing us to tie up at a state pier.

That afternoon the fog finally cleared and we opened the side chamber doors on the engine, pumped out the water and added oil. We filled the expansion tank and put water into the block chamber again and set out again for New Bedford. We arrived there in the early evening, running the crankshaft with water and oil—luckily without burning out the bearings.

When the engine was dismantled, we found the crankshaft in perfect condition and sold it for $200. We sold the old block to a junk dealer for $50. I shared up our earnings with the boys, including Tommy, who was only three years old. In New Bedford, we met Sonny Soares, a top-notch mechanic who befriended all of us and taught us some valuable lessons.

As it turned out, we would spend most of the summer months in New Bedford. I'd drive back to Gloucester every Friday morning to pick up Nina, who spent the weekends with us. We all slept in the fo'c'sle. Nina cooked great meals while we worked in the engine room and cleaned up after Sonny Soares and his crew left. I recall these days with great fondness. We were all working together to help ourselves.

By the first of September, the engine was installed and the boat looked fantastic. We had cleaned everywhere and painted the engine room, the fish hold and the fo'c'sle. The whole boat sparkled. I had kept the boys busy. Otherwise, they would have gotten bored.

We went out into the harbor for a trial run and were delighted with the results. We had more speed and a lot more power. Later, we would rig the *Linda B.* with heavier doors and bigger nets. It was very gratifying to have a good, sturdy boat under my feet once again. Even more satisfying was to have a crew made up of my sons.

THE IRON FISH

That fall, the three younger boys went back to school. Johnny and I handled the *Linda B.* until my brother-in-law Lawrence and his son Johnny came aboard.

We fished in Ipswich Bay and as far north as the Isles of Shoals, always setting out on the mud and sand near rocky bottoms with a chain net. I knew the depth and the texture of the ocean floor from years of towing back and forth on other boats. Our catches consisted mostly of flounder, cod, and haddock. Very few boats fished in the same areas I had staked out for the *Linda B.* These grounds were still unknown to most fishermen. Everything changed with the use of electronic LORAN and sophisticated sounding machines.

I'd hustle from one fishing spot to another, looking for the grounds where the fish could be found that day. It was more an art than a science. Soon enough, I was considered a high-liner (always catching my share of the fish) by the other day-boat skippers.

Each month I'd pay the mortgage notes, with interest, and an insurance premium for coverage on the men and boat. A third of the owner's share went to those two bills alone. The rest of the owner's share went to running the boat: ice, food, and gear came off the top first, then the balance of everything was shared equally among the men, crew and owner.

When Palm Sunday came along in 1958, I told the crew we'd stay in port. I rarely fished on Palm Sunday because I felt it was more important to go to church. To be truthful, I was far from a perfect

Catholic (I often missed Mass), but still, I believed in God and I always thought He understood me.

On this particular Palm Sunday, I would make an exception. I was on Fisherman's Wharf very early. The weather was calm and sunny. Everyone was going out to fish. Why should I stay in? I telephoned Nina. "Quick," I told her. "Go upstairs and wake up Johnny; we're going out."

By seven o'clock, Johnny, Lawrence and his son Johnny, and I were off the Isles of Shoals. We had the area to ourselves, and happily set out the nets. When we hauled back two hours later, we had one hell of a catch. The wire cables groaned with the weight. The *Linda B.* actually listed to the starboard side. I figured we had a rock or a piece of wreckage. We kept working the net out of the water depth with the winches. Johnny Scola peered over the side and shouted, "Stop! I think we got a small boat here. I can see the propeller."

I looked down and slowly recognized the outline of a big torpedo. It was caught in our nets. I immediately wished we all had gone to church instead. "Lower it down ten feet," I shouted, my mind racing with thoughts of the damn thing hitting the hull and blowing us all to smithereens. Fortunately, it had come up backwards, the twin propellers facing us and the nose away from the boat.

I went to the pilothouse and described the torpedo over the radio to the Boston Coast Guard. They told us to lower it away from the hull. I told them we had already done it. "Stand by. Help's on the way," they said.

I got another frequency and called my brother-in-law Captain Joe Randazza of the *Sandra Jean*, who was fishing twenty miles away. Telling Joe was like letting the whole fleet in on the delicate situation.

Next, I called the Boston marine operator and placed a call to my wife, knowing she would hear rumors about us and get scared. I explained to her we were all right and to tell Pauline the same. I didn't want either of them to be told of our situation by strangers. The story would spread rapidly through Gloucester.

I shut down the engine and we drifted northwesterly waiting for help. How are we going to get rid of this iron fish? Would it explode? Were we all goners? My mind was running a mile a minute.

The two cousins, Johnny and Johnny Scola, whispered between themselves while Lawrence chain smoked and kept repeating, "How are we going to get rid of this thing?"

It wasn't until two hours later that a Coast Guard patrol boat arrived with two navy demolition men. Each man was loaded with diving equipment when he came aboard. After an initial inspection of the torpedo, they ordered the Coast Guard to wait a mile away from us.

The demolition men donned diving gear and went below to inspect the torpedo. Meanwhile, the wind picked up from the southeast and gently rocked the *Linda B.* The divers would surface every few minutes and rest. One of them got sick and threw up. They both kept diving.

The demolition men told us the torpedo was live, clocked and ready to blow. My stomach did some strange things. Lawrence's face drained of color. I called the Coast Guard and told them to take my crew off the *Linda B.* Lawrence wanted me to get off with the others. "No," I said. "I can't leave these Navy men alone."

It probably was foolish of me not to get off with the rest of them. I really wasn't helping the situation any, but then again it was my boat. The Coast Guard took the crew more than a mile away from us. "How come they're going so far off?" I asked one of the divers.

"Captain, if this thing goes off, they wouldn't even find a little piece of this boat," he said. Strange things were happening to my stomach again. I felt even more queasy.

The winds continued to strengthen, and as we rolled and tossed, the wires strained the net. I wondered what was going to happen. After two more dives, the navy men came aboard again. One of them got on the radio and spoke to Boston. I had stayed in constant communication with Boston. "We can't hang on too much longer now," he said. "We're pitching back and forth."

Headquarters asked if we could cut loose the net and torpedo and put a buoy on it. "Yes, it can be done," we said.

I then became part of the demolition team. We worked fast, as dusk was approaching and the *Linda B.* was drifting toward a ridge of shoal water three miles away. As it was, we were only in seventy feet of water and the torpedo was eighteen feet long.

I tied a one-inch rope around the net and attached it to the forward gallast. We cut the wires to the net. Now all the weight of the torpedo and the net was on that one-inch line. We tied a second 300-foot rope around the net and attached a buoy to it.

I gave one of the divers a sharp knife and, at my signal, he was to cut the rope, leaving the *Linda B.* free of the torpedo. If all went right, the buoy would mark the torpedo.

"Cut," I screamed and opened the *Linda B.*'s throttle wide open. The boat, suddenly free of two tons of dead weight, took off like a wild horse, throwing a plume of black smoke behind us. I clutched the steering wheel so tightly that my hands were sore later. I looked into the faces of the navy men with fear in my heart, waiting for an explosion that never came.

Looking back, we saw the flag marking the spot where the "big fish" rested on the ocean's bottom. The commander said that the

torpedo, with the net attached to it, must have planed
off instead of going straight down, much to our relief.

Three days later, a navy tugboat arrived from New York City and
retrieved the torpedo, net, rope and flag buoy. The Coast Guard
returned my ruined gear to Fisherman's Wharf, where we were already
building a new net.

Nine months later, the federal government reimbursed us $300 for
the loss of a net and paid a hundred-dollar reward for finding the
torpedo. It took dozens of letters to Washington, written by Ellen
Kershaw, to get even this satisfaction.

The day after the ordeal, the *Gloucester Daily Times* had big
headlines about it. I think I aged ten years that day. When we arrived
home that night, all the family and relatives paid us a visit and
rejoiced at the escape we made from the deadly fish.

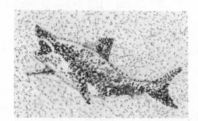

THOSE DAMN DOGFISH

June, 1960 was marked by a memorable occasion for the Testa-verde family. Salvatore became the first family member to graduate from high school and have a diploma. Nina and I barely got out of grammar school; all my brothers and sisters, and Nina's too, had quit school to take jobs. This was a first. As we watched with pride, Salvatore accepted his diploma from the high school principal. We had no idea that years later Salvatore would be working on his doctoral degree.

It wasn't a clean break from tradition, for Salvatore promptly took a job on the *Linda B.* fishing with his brother John and his cousin Salvatore Randazza.

The fishing in the early sixties had its ups and downs. Usually the trips we made were very profitable, sometimes just so-so, and occasionally they were downright bad. Fishing was like the weather in New England; it always changed. The one constant was that you had to go out and keep trying.

Lawrence fished on the *Linda B.* during the winter and spring, but went seining during the summer. He had been with me so long that his site was always guaranteed, no matter how many hands we had at the moment.

One September day we all got a lesson in what we called "the scourge of the fishermen," dogfish. They are a species of small shark. After towing off Rockport's Halibut Point for five miles, we hauled back a net full of five-foot-long sharks. With great disgust, we dumped our catch overboard and steamed another five miles north for another try. Half an hour later, we were again dumping dogfish over the side. A third try at towing in the same area produced the same sorry results.

We steamed to deeper water—fifty fathoms—and set out again. In twenty minutes, you guessed it, another net full of dogs. The cursing was vicious as we again dumped the bags over the side. By now it was late afternoon, and we hadn't caught a single marketable fish. We steamed another twenty miles, this time south, to "the hole" off Thatcher's Island. The boats *St. Providenza* and the *Eddie and Lulu* were already there.

I radioed the skippers of both boats. "Any dogfish?" I asked. "No, haven't had a dog yet," they said. *Finally we'll catch some fish*, I thought. So we set out for the fifth time. Even before hauling back, the skipper of the *St. Providenza* radioed that he had just picked up a load of dogfish. Strangely enough, it was the first they had caught all day. We knew we were destined to have another net full of flapping, useless dogfish. They were following the *Linda B.* wherever she went.

When we hauled back our fifth tow there was little doubt among the crew about what we would find. The good-for-nothing dogfish didn't let us down. We had caught 40,000 pounds of the lovely bastards all day. Our nets were all ripped up and our arms tired, all for nothing.

We cruised into Fisherman's Wharf at about five in the evening, with nothing to show for a full day's work. It was the first time in a lifetime of fishing on my boats that I had returned empty-handed. "How many boxes you need, Salve?" called "Joe Hem" Favazza, our maintenance man, as the *Linda B.* came alongside the wharf.

"None," I said, my temper about to explode.

"Come on, quit your kidding," Joe Hem said. "I gotta get the boxes from the storage room." Then Joe took a look at the hard, angry expression on my face and backed off. As my sons told Joe about the dogfish, he kept saying, "I don't believe it."

My pride wouldn't permit me to let go of this defeat. "Boys, I want you to go home, eat supper and come right back," I said. "I want to see you in one hour because we're going out fishing tonight." The boys had quizzical looks on their faces, but they marched off home without a word of protest. My plan was to try night fishing for cod on Middle Bank.

When the boys came back, Johnny said, "Mom says for you to come home and have supper before going out all night." My stomach was too knotted with frustration to eat. We worked all night and caught about 5,000 pounds of cod. As dawn approached, the boys were expecting me to steam home. I had a different idea.

"Now that we're out here, let's get another day's work done," I said as we steamed for a spot called the Half Hour. We set out our nets again and this time came up with fifty boxes of whiting. That afternoon we came in with ninety boxes, a total of 11,200 pounds of cod and whiting. Sure, we were tired and hungry, but satisfied. My determination had gotten us a trip. There was more than a few hundred dollars at stake that afternoon. The ocean always presented a challenge to me and I didn't want the ocean to get the best of me even for this one day. I attacked my job as if my life depended on it.

THE TESTAVERDE SCHOLAR

I was under the mistaken impression that Salvatore, the high school graduate, was happy in his work as a fisherman. My two younger sons, Joey and Tommy, would later graduate from high school and devote themselves happily to a life of fishing.

For Salvatore, there was a burning desire to use his mind more than his hands. Unfortunately, I didn't understand his ambitions, which led to an ugly incident.

We were towing between the humps and nearby rocky spots off the Isles of Shoals when Salvatore suddenly threw up his hands in disgust and announced he had quit. He was never particularly fond of fishing, especially in the cold winter months, but I never expected him to defy me while ten miles offshore.

As he stood knee-deep in a deck full of fresh-caught whiting, Salvatore's face became hard and cold as he repeated, "I quit." He stripped out of his rubber pants and boots and strode off to the bow, where he leaned against a railing. Then he pulled a cigarette from his pocket and started smoking, which startled me even more because I had forbidden him ever to smoke.

"Salvatore, help your uncle get the fish down below," I hollered from the pilothouse. He would not budge.

"I quit," he said. "This is slave work. And I'm not going to do it."

I shouldn't have left the wheel unattended, as we were near rocky bottom and playing a dangerous game of tag with the rocks. The net could easily have gotten caught in the rocks and "rimracked," or torn.

My temper, as usual, got the best of me and I risked losing the net by running down the deck and leaping at Salvatore like an animal.

I took hold of him by the scruff of his neck and ordered him to "pick up the goddamned fish." When he persisted in saying "This is slave work," I dragged him back to the pile of whiting and rubbed him in the fish. "This is the way I was brought up," I shouted, still holding him with one hand and rubbing the fish in his face with the other. "You work, work, work, or else you get nothing out of life and be damned forever."

He wouldn't listen, and he lashed out at me with his arms. I was wild and I gave him a backhand across the face. Blood spurted from his nose. At the sight of what I had done, my temper tantrum passed quickly. I tried to stem the flow of blood, but failed. We hauled back and rushed ashore. A broken vein in his nose had to be cauterized by a doctor.

Maybe it was frustration with my life of "work, work, work" that caused this outburst. Whatever it was, I am not proud of it in recalling my behavior. When Nina found out what had happened, she went into a rage of her own. It wasn't like her to blow up unless one of her children was mistreated. Then she became vicious. For days, she refused to speak to me. Salvatore stayed ashore for that week. My patience wore thin. Referring to him as *mangiafranco*, the Sicilian expression for "freeloader," I asked him if he was coming fishing with us.

"No," he said. He possessed a fair share of his father's stubbornness. I knew by the look in his eyes that it was time for me to back off. "Well then, " I said, "you go to work. What do you want to do?"

His words were slow and carefully measured. "I want to go to school and get a college education."

"Well, okay, " I said, "that's possible. First you have to work. Come back on the boat this summer, and then we'll see what we can do."

Salvatore returned to "slave work" and I kept my word, too. John Bennett, Sr., the high school chemistry teacher who had sold us the *Linda B.*, and a friend of his, a judge, came out fishing with us one day, just for the change of pace. I took the opportunity to sound out both of them about Salvatore's qualifications for school.

"Send him to school," John Bennett later told me. "He's got a good head on his shoulders. He needs a little sharpening up in chemistry. I'd be glad to tutor him." It was a very gracious offer, as John Bennett, Sr., never accepted a nickel for his hours of tutoring. He and his wife would come to our house every Friday night for three months. John and his student studied in the kitchen while Nina, Mrs.

Bennett and I watched television. When the books were put away, we'd all have coffee and cake.

Salvatore passed an entrance examination and enrolled at New Preparatory School in Cambridge. From there, he went on to Northeastern University and a wonderful career in fisheries science.

Salvatore paid his tuition from the money he earned fishing and the nest egg his mother had saved for him. Our desire for his success also helped him in many ways.

While in college, Salvatore somehow found out that *mangiafranco* translates to "freeloader." He was mad at me for days, and like his mother, refused to speak to me.

Salvatore earned a bachelor's degree in biology at Northeastern University. He continued to work on the *Linda B.* during the summers as he pursued a master's degree at Suffolk University. Eventually, he was awarded a Winston Churchill Travelling Fellowship to England. With an advanced degree, Salvatore began an exciting odyssey. He worked as a data analyst for the United States Bureau of Commercial Fisheries in Gloucester and on St. Simon Island, Georgia. He often worked aboard the decks of research vessels collecting data off the coast of Georgia, North Carolina and Florida. Of course, he was well acquainted with life at sea.

Salvatore's adventures continued in South America. In Colombia, he spent three years with the food and agriculture branch of the United Nations. Then he came home, first working at the New England Aquarium, then the state Division of Marine Fisheries.

Salvatore now works in the Gloucester office of the National Marine Fisheries Service. He is a resource policy analyst working closely with the Mid-Atlantic Fisheries Management Council. He's pursuing his doctoral degree from the University of New Hampshire. He and his wife, the former Joanne Scola, are the parents of a baby girl.

Mangiafranco, I'm proud of you.

When Salvatore graduated from Northeastern University, another first for the Testaverde family, Nina and I were again treated to a day of great pride. After the exercises, Salvatore and Joanne took Nina and me to dinner at a fancy Boston restaurant.

"Dad, how can I ever repay you?" Salvatore asked.

"Someday your mother and I are going to get old," I said. "all I want is for you to come by and see us. Just a simple 'Hello, Ma. Hello, Dad.' That's all I want."

THE DAY THE PRESIDENT WAS SHOT

I had to have a good reason to spend money in those days. A near collision with a freighter was a good enough reason. I was fishing that day with Salvatore, Johnny, Jackie Sutera and my nephew Salvatore Randazza. The fog was wicked, and we really shouldn't have gone out, but still we managed to edge our way past Dog Bar Breakwater and around Eastern Point Light.

The boys hit the bunks down below as I stood at the wheel and Johnny brewed a pot of coffee. I was busy fiddling with the depth-finder machine, trying to get it started, when my eye caught something shiny and bright in the fog bank. Sometimes you would see mirages in a fog bank. Could the light be land? I checked the compass. No, it wasn't land.

The realization that we had a ship bearing down on us hit me like a slap in the face. "'Damn, damn, damn," I muttered and pounded my fists on the wheel.

"Hey! Everyone on deck," I shouted behind me. "Everyone on deck right now." I turned the wheel hard over to starboard, not knowing that I was steering the *Linda B.* straight into the path of the oncoming monster ship. My confusion was caused by the fact that I couldn't see the ship's running lights, which are color-coded by starboard and port sides. If I had been able to see the lights, I would have been able to judge the ship's course and steer clear.

The ship's foghorn blared loud enough to shake the boys out of their bunks. Thank God the ship swept by us. She had only thirty feet of clearance, just missing us.

The *Linda B.* made a complete circle and veered off to the north-west. We headed straight in for the beach. When we were safely out of harm's way, I cut the engines. My legs were shaking. The boys came running up the ladder and asked what happened. I couldn't speak.

"Dad, that was a close one," said Johnny, who saw it all. He put a good slug of brandy in a cup of coffee and handed it to me. My shaking hands spilled the coffee until the brandy began to soothe my nerves. The boys stood around quietly on deck. After an hour of this drifting around, Johnny said, "Dad, are we going fishing or are we just going to lay here?"

"No," I replied. "We're not fishing today." I was getting old. In the old days, I would have shaken it off and kept fishing. Instead, we slowly groped through the thick fog back to the harbor and finally tied up at Fisherman's Wharf.

When Nina asked if we had gone out, I lied and told her I felt it was too dangerous even to leave the dock in this fog. Johnny and Salvatore were supposed to keep this close call a secret, too. Of course, it was impossible. Nina soon knew all the details. She always did.

The next day I was back to see my friends at the bank. I had to have $3,000 to buy a small RCA radar. I simply wasn't willing to invite another heart attack because a ship suddenly looms out of nowhere. A radar would allow me to calmly watch blips on a screen to know what ships are within six miles of us. I had to thank my sister-in-law Annie Randazza for backing me up on this latest loan. She put up the collateral. God bless the man who invented the radar. Today no fishing boat will leave the harbor without the radar and a spare.

In 1963, the assassination of President John F. Kennedy saddened the fishermen of Gloucester as it did people all around the world. We had our own reasons for championing the young President, for his people were also from a different land and had started out poor in this country.

Johnny and I came into the harbor late in the afternoon of that fateful day. We noticed a small group of people in an emotional discussion on the street corner as we walked toward home. "What's going on?" I asked.

"You haven't heard? The President's been shot."

"Oh my God," I murmured and hurried home, finding Nina in the kitchen, her face wan and her eyes red.

"Salve, they've shot the President and he's dead," she said, bursting into tears. We huddled in front of the television. All the flags on the waterfront wharves and on the boats were lowered to half-mast. As a rule, fishermen weren't interested in politics. Many didn't bother with the newspapers; some couldn't even read English. We were all out fishing too often to make a regular habit of voting. President Kennedy was still special to us. We knew he cared about the poor and we always considered ourselves the poor. We all felt as if we had lost a member of the family.

"PROFESSOR" TESTAVERDE

I had a liberal policy about taking guests out on the *Linda B.* and wound up playing host to scientists, professors and newspaper reporters. Once I had to turn away the attractive wife of a reporter. She was wearing a dress, and I was afraid she'd be a distraction to the boys.

Once my sons and I lectured to a crowd of seventy students from Cornell University. The lecture was held at a marine laboratory run by Cornell on the Isles of Shoals. Dr. Kingsbury was the head of the project. The *Linda B.* had come ashore at the island for shelter during bad weather. Dr. Kingsbury asked if the students could make an inspection of a working fishing boat. "Of course," I said, and welcomed them aboard.

Before long, I found myself delivering a lecture to the students. Thereafter, we would make regular stops at the laboratory for more talks and to bring in specimens. Salvatore, by now a marine biologist himself and aboard the *Linda B.* for the summer, spoke the same language as the students and made a big hit with them.

On later visits, we showed homemade movies that demonstrated the different types of fishing we did aboard the *Linda B.* After the lecture periods, we'd all have refreshments. These were very pleasant experiences.

One morning I shocked a crowd of students with my old-world habits. Walking a small specimen pond, I spotted a big sea urchin. Without thinking, I picked up the sea urchin, cut it open, and popped the meat into my mouth. "Salve, you're going to die of poisoning," said a horrified professor.

"If I'm going to die by eating a sea urchin, there wouldn't be any Italians, Spaniards, French or Greeks alive today. All Mediterraneans eat sea urchins. It's a delicacy. Here, do you want to try some?"

"No way," he said. On a visit four years later, I found students eating sea urchins, periwinkles and mussels. I guess my initiation got them started on some of the great delicacies of the sea.

My casual relationship with the Isles of Shoals group led to an invitation from Dr. West of Suffolk University. Salvatore and I narrated fishing films to a group of forty high school teachers who had come from all over the country to take advanced courses in marine biology. Considering my limited education, this kind of attention was like a feather in my cap.

Many newspaper reporters wrote stories based on their experiences aboard the *Linda B*. Some came to write about the Russian trawlers which were raping our fish stocks in the sixties and early seventies. Others came to write about the Gloucester way of life. The *Boston Record-American*, the *Boston Globe*, New York's *Herald Tribune*, *The Wall Street Journal*, *The Christian Science Monitor*, and the *Gloucester Daily Times* all sent reporters.

The federal government even got into the act. The National Marine Fisheries Service had me take out visiting scientists from Washington and even two men from Togo, Africa. I was first contacted by officials at the local branch of the Bureau of Commercial Fisheries. They asked me if I would take observers from another country on board during their visit to the United States. I said yes.

My guests turned out to be a master fisherman and a consul from Togo. The fisherman was short and looked just like Louis Armstrong. The government man was tall, thin and dignified-looking. They were visiting this country in hopes of learning new methods of fishing in order to improve catches in their country, which needed the food very badly. They were interested in gill netting, pot fishing, and, of course, dragging, which is what I was doing at the time. I think, however, during our trips that I learned as much about them as they did about me and our fishing methods.

Our first day out began at two o'clock in the morning from Fisherman's Wharf. The fog was thick and both men were startled when I told the crew to cast off. My guests stood on deck and appeared amazed as I steered out of the harbor. I suspect they had heard of radar but they had never seen it in operation. I showed them all the electronics including the sonar and sounding depth machine.

When we arrived at the fishing grounds, visibility was still very limited in the fog. My crew set out the net and I proceeded to tow. Both men joined me in the pilothouse while my crew all went below to sleep. I explained everything I knew about the gear, the fish finder and dragging. The fisherman and I talked about other things, too. He even told me he had four wives.

Our first set was not so good, 4,000 pounds of mostly trash fish, which the crew quickly sorted out on deck. My son John waded through the catch, throwing the so-called "junk" fish, such as dogfish, herring, ling and skates, overboard. The master fisherman got all excited and rushed to grab John's arm as he worked. "What's the matter with you people? First you catch them, then you throw them away!" he yelled. "These are trash fish," I cut in; "the American public won't eat them."

He shook his head and explained that in his country nothing goes to waste. He told us that when his countrymen fish, the whole catch, net and all, is dragged on shore, usually at a beach, and the natives come down the same day and pick it over. They had no refrigeration, and the fish spoiled quickly in the sun. He was here to learn, but perhaps the bigger lesson is the one I got about how lucky we were here.

At day's end we unloaded more than forty boxes of mixed fish. By our standards, we made some money, but not much. The Togo fisherman tempted me when he told me that if we should land the same catch in his country, we would be very important and also very wealthy.

The *Linda B.* was a box fishing operation during these years. All our catches were packed at sea. Fish species had to be culled and packed, on ice, into wooden boxes. When we hit shore, the nailed-tight boxes would be ready for shipping by truck to New York. The *Linda B.* could handle fifty-five boxes in the hold and another twenty on deck.

Often we'd throw a lot of fish over the side, including everything under three pounds and the junk fish—because of its price—including whiting, hake, ling, monkfish and squid. We had no room for it. One man's junk was another man's living.

Because of the size of the *Linda B.* I had to fish for the "money fish": cod, haddock, flounder. Many of the boats in the Italian fleet fished for whiting. To make a profitable catch of whiting, you needed a boat that could carry at least 50,000 pounds; otherwise the two-cents-a-pound price just didn't add up to much. The *Linda B.*'s capacity was only 22,000 pounds. We filled our precious space with only the highest-per-pound values.

Johnny found the disposal of perfectly good fish very frustrating and kept hounding me to buy a new boat. In fact, he already had a $100,000 boat picked out for me. "No, I'll never buy another boat," I said. I had been in debt too long to take another deep plunge. The *Linda B.* was profitable and I intended to keep the boat, and my life, on a nice, even keel. There would be no more big risks for me. My greatest satisfaction came from being able to fish with my sons. I was a happy man and wasn't interested in throwing the dice on the future.

I was interested in reducing my debts. My insurance premium was $2,500 a year, yet I owed only $1,800 on the boat. This seemed way out of whack to me. I figured I'd take a chance and drop my insurance altogether. The bank wouldn't hear of it. They were not going to take any risks on their precious $1,800. I had a big argument with the bank vice president and took all my banking business across the street.

I then remortgaged the house for a $5,000 loan, paid off the $1,800 and canceled the insurance policy with a few choice words. The extra $3,200 went into the boat, including an overhaul, a new LORAN and a new radar. I felt like a new man, a free man. Finally I began to act more shrewdly in my business dealings. The money I saved on the canceled insurance policy went directly to the bank. I shoved all my earnings over the expenses into the reserve fund, for emergencies. Some weeks, a couple hundred went into the bank; other weeks, not so much.

By 1965, Johnny's admonitions about buying a bigger boat led me to find a more innovative solution to our problems. I wouldn't sell the *Linda B.*; I'd make it bigger. My plan was to cut the *Linda B.* in half, insert a new section and mend her up again. The 52-foot *Linda B.* would become the 60-foot *Linda B.*

Harry Cusick, the manager of Gloucester Marine Railways, and I measured the boat up and down, and then he announced a price of $7,500. He said he'd add eight feet to the length of the *Linda B.*, build new ribs and stanchions and deepen the keel by another six inches. "That includes everything," he said. "Put it all in writing," I quickly said. He did and we signed a contract.

The next day I checked my reserve fund and was astonished to find I had over $12,000. I could cover the work and put down deposits on still another new LORAN and still another, bigger, more powerful radar. Those two pieces alone would cost $8,000. This was one hell of a big splurge. The whole boat was totally remodeled. What the heck, I figured, you had to spend money to make money.

Dozens of people watched as the marine railways workmen cut up the *Linda B.* and put her back together. It was a novelty. Only one other boat—the *Jeannne D'Arc*, I think—had been lengthened in this manner in Gloucester.

While the *Linda B.* was drydocked, I grabbed a site with my good friends Captain Tony Bertolino and Jackie Lombardi on the dragger *Santa Lucia*. I was a crew member but often volunteered to cook, to kill time. These were happy times among friends, and I fattened up the crew with my cooking. Whenever we were in port because of windy weather, I'd be at the boatyard to inspect the work on the *Linda B*.

In late spring, my boat was returned to me. She was freshly painted and had a new, three-ton cement ballast holding her steady. My sons and I were delighted with the results. Not only was the fish hold capacity doubled, the *Linda B*. now was also a more seaworthy boat. We could stow ninety-two boxes in the hold and another thirty-odd on deck, though there were very few trips when we needed every inch of capacity.

The price was a bargain, too. This work today would cost more than $50,000. Harry Cusick later told me that he lost money on the deal. He said he took the job only to keep his men working during the usually idle winter season.

Two men could handle the *Linda B*. Johnny and I concentrated on groundfish—cod and flounder—and brought in as much as ninety boxes a day. Oh, we were in the money again. Johnny and I were doing the work of four men. I didn't mind the hard work because I had new plans now. My dream was going to come true. When school ended that June, Salvatore, fourteen-year-old Joey and nine-year-old Tommy joined Johnny and me on the boat.

Finally, the crew was comprised entirely of my sons. We fished as a family unit. That summer we worked practically every day on the whiting fishery, getting eight cents a pound for the fish we once considered junk and threw overboard. During that summer alone, I earned back every nickel I had invested in the *Linda B*.

Trip after trip, we'd come in with a minimum of 30,000 pounds of whiting. The best trips brought 48,000 pounds which figured out to a hefty gross of almost $4,000. I had never made so much money. Best of all, every cent stayed in the family, which was expanding. Johnny and his wife, Jean Codinha, had begun a family of their own. Nina acted as our treasurer, wisely saving for the three younger boys' futures.

With all my bills paid off, it was time to spend some money again. More modern navigational equipment came aboard. After all, the fish finders, LORANs and radars had paid for themselves, allowing us to get out of port in rain, snow, or fog, and helping us locate and stay with the fish. The fish finders used sonar to pick up the density of fish massed in great schools. Now I had two of everything electronic. I shook my head in disbelief when thinking about the old days of living hand-to-mouth and borrowing from relatives.

I was a happy man, indeed, but the future clouded with the report that Nina wasn't feeling well. The doctor diagnosed her as diabetic. She had to have a special diet and insulin shots every morning. Nina's mother was a diabetic, too, but lived well into her seventies by strictly following doctor's orders.

With all the boys fishing with me that summer, Nina was home alone and grew bored. Without my knowledge or approval, she took a job in one of the local fish plants, packing whiting. One of her sisters and a few of her friends worked there. She'd hurry home every night to beat me in the door and keep her secret.

By fall, the younger boys were back in school, and Johnny and I had the boat to ourselves again. When I came home to dinner one evening, Nina wasn't there. Joey and Tommy said she had gone to a show at the North Shore Theater and that my supper was already in the oven. In the old days, when I was a kid, an Italian woman wouldn't go out without her husband, mother, or sister. Times had changed, and I certainly didn't mind her going to a show.

I decided to wait for Nina because we always ate our dinner together. Three hours later, I was still waiting. I pumped Joey and Tommy for answers and found out she had been working at the fish plant for two months. I was furious. Ten minutes later, Nina strolled in the door, stinking like hell of old, very ripe, fish. "Go take a bath," I snapped. "Then I want to talk to you."

When she came downstairs, I started to give her hell. "What's the matter, all these years haven't I supported you? Now you have to go to work?"

"When you're out and I'm alone, I get bored in the house day after day, so that's why I went to work, just to get out of the house," she said.

My temper faded. "But why do you have to work at night? I want you home when I come home so we can talk and eat dinner together."

"Tonight it was an emergency," she said. "They were shorthanded at the plant and paid double time to get the orders filled."

"Just make it days in the future," I said, resigned. For the next couple of years, Nina would work during the summer whiting season and knock off each October. Meanwhile, the years came and went as the boys grew up on the *Linda B.* Soon, Joey and Tommy were in high school.

In 1972, we almost lost the *Linda B.* in a sudden squall off Wingaersheek Beach. We had picked up 3,000 pounds of cod in one set off the Isles of Shoals when the northern sky turned almost black with big, puffy clouds. "Wait a minute, Johnny," I said, "let's not set out again until we know what this weather is going to do."

I was afraid of being belted by a sudden gale of wind. I had seen it happen before. Joe Marcantonio, a friend of my son, and Johnny hauled back the net in five minutes. Already we had winds over thirty miles an hour. I opened the throttle for the mouth of the Annisquam River, sixteen miles away. We weren't alone in running for shelter. The whole fleet was plowing across Ipswich Bay for the river, too.

The seas were terrific as the *Linda B.* rose and fell with the swells. Only two miles from the river, the *Linda B.* became disabled. I was steering to the starboard but the *Linda B.* was headed in the opposite direction. I figured the rudder had pivoted and snapped off. I immediately threw the clutch out of gear and turned the steering wheel again, to no avail. I told Johnny to go the stern and look overboard. "The rudder's still there, Dad," he called back. "I can see it."

We had a rudder, but it was useless. It seemed the rudder shaft and blade had loosened in all the pounding. All that could be figured out later. Right now I had to work out a way to get into the river without a rudder to steer. The coastline, some of it rocky, was getting closer as we drifted helplessly. The wind made a frightening howl and the seas smashed us. I spotted the *Cigar Joe*, captained by Busty Frontiero, coming astern of us. I radioed Busty to heave us a line and tow us in, but it was no good. The *Linda B.* was too heavy for the *Cigar Joe* in these rolling seas.

Another, larger boat approached. It was the 65-foot dragger *Acme*, captained by John Cusumano. I told Busty to cut the line and run for shelter. Then I radioed Captain Cusumano about our crisis. Meanwhile, I had radioed the Coast Guard to send help. No rescue boats were available, as the storm had caught and overturned a dozen sailboats. "Stand by," they said.

"We can't stand by," I radioed back. "We're drifting fast toward the beach." Soon, the Gloucester police boat, captained by Keith Trefry, raced out of the Annisquam River in an attempt to get to us, but was forced back by the heavy seas.

Johnny, Joe and I rigged a 120-foot line of rope and tossed it over the seas to the crew of the *Acme*. The line was fastened and held the *Linda B.* from drifting up on the beach. Still, we were too heavy to be towed.

A long hour and a half later, the Coast Guard finally reached us in a 30-foot boat, about the size of a lobster boat. I complained bitterly to station headquarters that the boat was too small to tow us. We had to take what we had. We cut the line to the *Acme* and thanked the captain for his help. Without the *Acme*, we probably would have lost the boat—and maybe our lives—on those rocks.

The Coast Guard took us in tow with a 600-foot rope. We could not use the river and had to go all the way around Cape Ann, just barely crawling along; our weight was too much for the little Coast

Guard boat. Conditions worsened. In all the years I fished Ipswich Bay, I had never seen the seas so rough. Northeast winds were over fifty miles an hour. As the seas came crashing over the bow and deck, I told Johnny and Joe to get the life preservers and the life raft and bring everything into the pilothouse. "And lock the fo'c'sle door," I yelled. "I want everyone together if worse comes to worse."

It took us eight hours to get around the Cape. Under normal conditions, a boat can be towed the distance in less than two. When we arrived at Fisherman's Wharf, my family and Joe's were waiting.

TOURISTS

In 1970, Nina and I took another vacation. It was our first in twenty-two years. I left Johnny and the other boys to take the boat out, and off we flew to Portugal for a month. We were accompanied by my sister Rosie and her husband, Tony DaCruz, who hadn't seen his mother and father in more than twenty years.

We stayed at the DaCruz family home in Ilhavo, 150 miles north of Lisbon on the Atlantic coast. It was a beautiful sixteen-room villa, surrounded by orchards of orange, tangerine, and lemon trees, all enclosed by a wall. Here I got the flavor of the old country that my parents spoke of so often. I have still never been to Italy.

Day after day we visited all over the country in two hired Volkswagens—seeing the cities of Aveiro, Porto, Braga and Coimbra, the "city of colleges." We paid homage to the sacred Shrine of Our Lady of Fatima outside Lisbon. At the seaport of Setubal, just below the capital city, we observed the gillnetting, longlining, and seining fisheries. Fishermen sold their catches in open-air markets on the beach. We had a wonderful time observing the different customs on the other shore of the Atlantic. We bought gifts and jewelry for the grandchildren and Nina's family.

Soon, we were off on another trip, this time to visit Salvatore and Joanne in Colombia. I loved to travel and now, just getting past middle age, I was determined to see as much of the world as I could. Besides, for the first time, I could afford to travel. I had Johnny take the boat out again. He was as reliable as the tide. I could relax with him taking care of the family business.

Salvatore worked out of Cartagena, an Atlantic Ocean port near Panama, and I was thrilled to find eighty-degree temperatures waiting for us there. With all the tropical plants around, I thought I was in paradise. Salvatore warned me that I was seeing only half the picture. He took me to a crowded, open-air marketplace in the middle of the city where the natives were. People were so poor and conditions so filthy that my stomach retched. I wanted to leave. "There are only two classes of people here," Salvatore told me quietly, "the very rich and the very poor." I knew exactly what he meant. I could see it in the dirt streets in front of me.

We, however, lived at the end of a long, sandy peninsula, in a seventh-floor apartment at the Towers by the Sea. Salvatore leased seven rooms from a rich Colombian who was in the United States on business. The cost of living was cheap here, just as it had been in Portugal. The American dollar worked hard in these poor countries. Salvatore paid only a dollar and fifteen cents to the maid for a day's work. The Towers was a fourteen-floor skyscraper overlooking the ocean with a big swimming pool in front. No question about it, we were with the rich.

The temperature reached ninety-five degrees without my feeling it. I loved burying myself in the beach sand and baking away the aches and pains from home.

Salvatore's bosses invited Nina and me to Bogotá, the capital city, 600 miles inland. We all flew to this city that is 9,000 feet above sea level and surrounded by still higher peaks of the Andes Mountains. The four million people of Bogotá live in a long, bowl-shaped valley. The hundreds of tall building there reminded me of New York City.

We stayed at the Presidential Hotel in Bogotá. Nina and I had a two-bedroom apartment across from Salvatore and Joanne. The rooms were very clean. Everything was perfect. We had three days of dining and drinking and stayed busy with all the sights and shopping. We also made the acquaintance of Salvatore's bosses and friends.

One night I drank a few highballs and ate a heavy meal. The next day Joanne led Nina and me on a walking tour to the gold museums and art galleries. After three hours of walking, I suddenly felt as if I couldn't breathe anymore. I was standing in an open public garden just outside one of the galleries when my head started to spin. I felt as if someone was shoving my head in the water and keeping it there. I sat down on a bench and gasped. Joanne and Nina, who had walked on ahead, turned around and became alarmed at the sight of me gagging.

I was rushed back to the hotel by cab. Secretly, I thought I was having a heart attack. The hotel doctor gave me a whiff of oxygen and I snapped out of it. He said strangers often make the mistake of eating and drinking too heavily in Bogotá. It's the altitude, he said. It causes heart attacks, sometimes fatal ones. I took it easy on the highballs and double helpings after that.

We flew back to Cartagena and stayed there for another three weeks. We were at sea level now and the breathing was easier. We enjoyed sunning ourselves next to the pool and on the beach.

The four of us went gift shopping one evening at a modern department store. It looked like a slightly exotic Woolworth's. One thing didn't fit. Lying in the doorway of the store were three or four small boys, none older than four years. They were sleeping, all curled up in little balls against the wind. A little redheaded boy struck Nina's fancy. He was fast asleep, with his thumb in his mouth. Salvatore said the boys were homeless. They had to fend for themselves. We started to walk again but Nina took pity on this little redhead and said, "Salve, let's adopt him."

Salvatore explained they were under the protection of the Colombian government, and adoption wouldn't be allowed. The boy woke up as we looked down at him. There was no expression on his face. I gave him an American half dollar. Salvatore gave me hell. "You do that and they'll follow you home and stand outside your door all night," he said. Salvatore took the half dollar from the kid and gave it back to me. "Let's go," he said.

As we turned to leave, I saw Salvatore slip the boy a dollar bill. He was trying to hide it from me. I'm glad I saw him. I knew my son wasn't cruel. I knew he had a heart.

TRADITIONS

Johnny had proven himself a fine captain again and again as I traveled around the world. I made the mistake of taking back the boat when I returned. I should have kept Johnny behind the wheel of the *Linda B.* and found another boat for myself, or I could have become the crew for my son. Being shuffled from captain to crew was not good for Johnny's confidence. I remembered how I'd had to win my own father's trust by taking the boat out behind his back, and I regretted what I was doing to my own son.

We fished Middle Bank for groundfish, and all the way up the coast of Maine for flounder. The routine had been established long ago. We were asleep by nine at night, up by two in the morning, and on the fishing grounds by dawn. We usually came in around five o'clock in the evening. Sometimes we stayed out too long, and slept on the boat, which we tied up in Folly Cove or in York Harbor, Maine. We'd buy a dinner of fried clams and ice cream from the little restaurants on the piers. It was like a night out for us. We were the only tourists to arrive at the popular roadside spots by boat. In the morning we would slip directly into Ipswich Bay and start fishing again.

Once at the Folly Cove pier I made a pair of wonderful friends. Lester and Hattie Blankley were visiting Gloucester and Rockport from Leeds, New York, which is in the Catskill Mountains. We got to talking and I eventually agreed to take them out fishing on a dare. They looked like ordinary city people and they seemed so nice, I was willing to take them through the rough and tumble of a fishing trip.

The Blankleys came back to Gloucester every summer and came aboard the *Linda B.* many times. They became old hands on the boat. In the evenings, Nina and I took them around to places to eat and to see Cape Ann's most spectacular natural sights. Nina and I also accepted their gracious hospitality in Leeds. Through the years, they watched as Joey, Tommy and the grandchildren grew.

I saw fewer friends regularly as I grew older. My friendships were deeper now, bonding together whole families. My brother-in-law Joe Randazza introduced me to Tommy Gangi, who owned the T.G. Fish Company in New York. Tommy's sons, Frankie, Rossi and Tommy, Jr., were in the family business. The Testaverdes and Gangis became good friends.

I met Tommy while looking for a fish broker in New York. There were a lot of sharpies down there who were in the habit of sending back nothing for your fish. You had to find someone you could trust a business partner whose principles were based on a firm shake of the hand. Nothing had to be written; no lawyers were needed—just a simple understanding.

Joe Randazza, my wife's brother, fished all winter out of New York and knew the Fulton Market dealers; he tipped me off that Tommy was coming to Gloucester on business. We met and talked. "Tommy, you treat me right and I'll get you all the fish you can handle," I said. Already, I had a good feeling about this guy. "No splits with the other dealers," I continued; "you get every fish, every trip. You can count on only top-rate fish."

Tommy said, "Try me," and I did. From then on, I shipped all my fish to the T.G. Fish Company. The price was always good. Our business partnership was mutually beneficial. More than that, a kinship grew. Over the next twenty years, we watched all the boys, his and mine, grow.

Tommy, Sr. died several years ago, but his son Rossi took over the business and continued to treat us well. I'm retired now, and although my sons ship to several dealers, they still give the Gangis a piece of the action.

During all this, my boys all took charge of their futures. Joey graduated from high school and went on to Franklin Institute in Boston, studying architectural engineering. Like Salvatore, he always had a summer and part-time job aboard the family boat. There were very few college freshmen with better-paying jobs than Salvatore's or Joey's. Tommy quit high school and enrolled at ITT Technical School in Chelsea for auto mechanics. He got his diploma and worked in a local garage before returning to fishing. Johnny, Joey and Tommy are all captains of their own boats today.

A BARGE IN THE WAY

The next incident aboard the *Linda B.* gave us quite a jolt. I had Johnny, Joey and Tommy Frontiero with me when we plowed into an unlighted barge anchored in the channel leading to Blynman Cut.

We were headed for cod and flounder fishing in northern Ipswich Bay in December, 1975. From Gloucester Harbor to the bay, you could either go twelve miles around Cape Ann or five miles through the cut and up the Annisquam River. In the pilothouse, I had snapped on the radar and was waiting for it to warm up as we glided by the old Cape Ann Fisheries building in the Fort. I called ahead to Blynman Bridge tender Salvatore Brancaleone to open up for us. I yelled for Johnny to get the spotlight and find the buoys for me as we made the river channel and rounded the bend for the Cut.

Joey and Tommy were down below in the fo'c'sle making coffee and talking away as we rounded the greasy pole stage that was used during the St. Peter's Fiesta. The bridge was beginning to open. I had been doing this for fifty years.

When I saw the green lights atop the bridge span, I pushed the throttle to nine knots speed, knowing I'd have to fight the channel current under the boat. Suddenly, I heard Johnny yell, "Put it in reverse! Put it in reverse!" I lost precious seconds not understanding him. The lights from the bridge and boulevard were glaring in my eyes. Then I saw it.

I yanked the wheel hard to port and threw the throttle out. It just lay there for us: a fully loaded 150-foot barge straight across the channel. It was anchored just as if it belonged there.

The *Linda B.* splintered when it took the full force of the barge. Johnny and his spotlight went flying fifteen feet in the air and landed against the winch. Joey was thrown off the ladder he was climbing and landed on Tommy. I saw it coming and braced myself. The collision thumped me against the wheel. Thank God I didn't go through the window.

The *Linda B.* rolled thirty degrees to port. Floorboards popped loose from the frame. We were immediately taking on water. Johnny almost slid off the pitched deck. He couldn't get up because his back was injured. He grabbed the scupper hole. His arm went through the hole and plunged into the water. Poor Johnny thought the boat was going to roll over on him. He had a nervous shake for three days. He held on there on the edge of the deck until we could get to him.

A nephew, Captain Johnny Randazza of the dragger *Debbie Rose*, answered our distress call. He called the Coast Guard. The fo'c'sle had already filled with two feet of water. At this rate, we'd lose her, bow first, in about thirty minutes, right in the middle of the Cut.

My first reaction was to beach her about 1,000 feet away on Pavilion Beach. I was frantic to get her out of the deep water of the channel. The boat's lights had been knocked out. Following the glow of the flashlight, we made our way down to the fo'c'sle, only to find it flooding fast.

Joey got an electric pump going. It was no use. The water was rising faster that than the pump could pump. Johnny checked the fish hold. It was dry. The bulkhead between the fo'c'sle and the fish hold held. Only the fo'c'sle was flooded, for the time being at least. Five tons of ice lying against the bulkhead helped absorb the impact.

I grabbed the microphone and cut into the Coast Guard to talk with my nephew. "I'm taking on water fast; I'm heading for Fisherman's Wharf," I cried.

I had to get the *Linda B.* drydocked to save her from sinking. All kinds of things went through my head. I had no insurance. I had to save our boat.

The microphone gave me a hell of a zap. That was the tip-off to some serious electrical problems. When I had turned the steering wheel with all my might, the steel cable jammed and parted a wire. Now the wire was lying across two banks of thirty-two-volt batteries. The boat was shorting out and had no steering.

I got a four-foot Stillson wrench and rigged it to the rudder shaft to get us home. I fitted the wrench to the big nut on the shaft so it turned one way or the other to guide us through the inner harbor. I stood on deck relaying the orders down to the boys, who turned the wrench. The stove was hissing as the water poured over it in the fo'c'sle.

All the radio chatter had attracted a big crowd of fishermen to the wharf for our arrival. Coast Guard and police boats came alongside us and dropped off pumps. More pumps were put to use. Our electric pump burned out as the water rose to the ceiling and trickled into the fish hold. Another pump came aboard. The fire department was called because we had little flash fires in the engine room. Batteries, wires and a switching board were strewn together in a pile.

Not far from the electrical flashes were four tanks holding 1,600 gallons of fuel oil. The impact had thrown the tanks off their braces, rupturing the fuel lines and spilling fuel into the bilge. We put still another pump into the engine room bilge to draw off that oil. An explosion or fire could have come at any moment.

To our astonishment, the firemen stopped us from pumping the oil into the harbor. They said we might catch the docks on fire. What a ticklish situation we had. We pumped the oil and bilgewater into five-gallon cans and did jackass work for three hours, carrying those cans around. Then Johnny got a long hose with a nipple, joined it to the pump line, and slipped it over the side. We pumped the oil and bilge-water below the water's surface and saved our backs.

It took three months to get the *Linda B.* back in tip-top shape again. The stem had been split clean in two and the cover boards between the stanchions were cracked the whole sixty-foot length of the boat. On top, the fifty-foot wooden mast was snapped off. The engine had to be readjusted and rebolted to the floor timbers. I needed $15,000 to repair her. And me with no insurance.

Almost from the moment of impact, I knew this would be a lawsuit. I'd need lots of good photographs and a smart lawyer. I thought I was home free because the Coast Guard, local police, and bridge tender verified that the barge had no lights. The next day, however, the barge was mysteriously moved out of the channel. The owners would later claim that it was never in the channel.

I lost a winter's work and paid the $15,000 in railways bills out of my emergency fund, thinking I'd get promptly reimbursed by the barge owners. Johnny went to a doctor for his back a couple of times, then said the hell with it. I tried to convince him to have his back checked out carefully, but he was stubborn about it and refused to go.

I wanted my lawyer to attach a lien on the company doing the construction work at the new Coast Guard station. Maybe we could get a bond posted against damage to my boat. Not a chance. Some kind of complicated leasing arrangement between the general contractors and the barge company protected both.

I think I got shafted. The barge company's lawyer was an ex-lieutenant in the Coast Guard. He tried to crack me during questioning for an affidavit at the base. I held up against him. I could see how he was trying to trip me up. My lawyer reported back to me that the barge owners had no assets, no insurance, no nothing. The whole thing dragged out over three years before the case was settled out of court for only $12,000. The lawyer took a third of that, leaving me with a grand total of $8,000. I gave $1,000 to Johnny for the aggravation to his back. I had no choice but to settle. I was running out of money and had bills to pay.

I did manage one small victory. I talked myself out of a $600 fine for not having a proper lookout on the bow. When the Coast Guard commander tried to lay that on me, I exploded and jumped to my feet. We were in his Boston office, and the sting of the collision had not worn off yet.

"What do you mean by that?" I hollered. "My boy Johnny was up on the bow, ten feet away from the bow stem with nothing to obstruct his view. If he hadn't shouted, we probably would have all been killed!"

The commander calmly answered that a proper lookout stands at the peak of the bow and looks out ahead. My lawyer tried to restrain me, but I ignored him, and jumped to my feet again. "You tell me the difference between a lookout standing exactly at the bow stem and the one standing ten feet away, with nothing to obstruct his view, when there's a barge with no lights sitting in the channel," I shouted. "And how about boats that have only two men? How are they supposed to have a proper lookout when one is in the pilothouse and the other's getting the engine running right? And how about your government boats that I see going out of the harbor with no one on the bow?" He didn't like this last question.

"If that barge didn't anchor there, none of this would have happened. Don't blame me. I'm like a blind man. I can go through all the rooms without touching anything in the dark, knowing where I am all the time. You rearrange the furniture and I'll stumble. Fifty years I've been going through the river in the night, in mist, in fog, with no accidents. You go ahead and fine the barge company, not me."

I realized my lawyer was holding my arm, trying to sit me down. The commander said nothing. A couple of seconds went by. "Testaverde," he said finally, "I'm going to let you off. Dismissed."

When we were in the car, my lawyer said, "Salve, you were wonderful." A week later, the Coast Guard sent me a citation for not having a proper lookout. The fine was waived. They were just trying to save face. Today, Johnny still walks with a limp because of his back.

THE LIFE OF LEISURE

Nina and I had set aside enough money to enable us to take a vacation in Hawaii. She was carefully treating her diabetes, but still she wasn't feeling well. The trip to Hawaii helped lift her spirits. We spent eight days and seven nights there. We took in the sights, baked in the hot sun, and went nightclubbing. Nina's sister Mamie and her husband went with us.

We were trying to make up for time lost throughout the years, when there was never enough money to get away for even an evening. I had Johnny, Joey, and Tommy on the boat now. Joey had married Joanne Puccio on May 12, 1974, and had settled down to make a steady living. Two years later, on May 28, 1976, Tommy married Roseanne Curcuru.

The boys didn't need me. I was getting old now. Nina and I joined a group of friends and relatives on a Caribbean cruise aboard the *Michelangelo*, a 47,000-ton Italian luxury liner. Every night we gambled and went to clubs. I was a little surprised by Nina's thrill at playing the slot machine.

I took a whack at the blackjack table and was winning big until the dealers changed. I ended up losing forty dollars. It was a fine time anyway. The buffet tables were piled high with food every night, for midnight dinners. At Barbados, Martinique and St. Thomas, Nina went shopping for gifts and jewelry for the family. We returned to New York after two weeks of this paradise.

We also drove out to Eagle, Wisconsin, with my brother Peter and his wife, Jenny, to see my niece Rose Marie. We took forty pounds of fresh fish with us and cooked monkfish and catfish filets for Rose Marie's family and friends. Peter, a gourmet cook, made ten large pizzas. The food was a big hit with everyone. These midwesterners wanted to know what kind of fish I was serving. "It's angelfish," I lied, knowing they might not be so impressed with monkfish and catfish.

"It's out of this world," they said.

"I know, that's why they call it angelfish," I said with a twinkle in my eye.

The next day, four of the men asked Peter and me about taking a shot at a fish and pizza restaurant there in Wisconsin. "You can't go wrong," they said. "People will come from miles around for fish like that. And pizza, too." Peter and I just laughed it off, but if we'd been younger, who knows?

NINA'S TROUBLE

When we returned home from our most recent trip, Johnny said, "Take the wheel, Dad. It belongs to you." I became absorbed in my work again and didn't recognize Nina's failing health.

She would wipe the table with a sponge and miss whole sections of it. When I came home one evening from fishing, I noticed tomato juice splattered all over the wood panel walls in the kitchen. I asked her what had happened and she said, "What do you mean?"

"What's wrong?" I asked angrily. "Nina, look at the walls and ceiling. They're all plastered with tomato juice. Look at it." She quickly composed herself, trying to keep her secret from me.

"Oh, Salve, I opened a can of tomatoes and must have splashed them," she said. With that, I dismissed the subject. Two weeks later, I asked her for a cup of coffee. She poured the coffee on my wrist. I hollered and yelled, "What's the matter with you?"

"I missed the cup, Salve, that's all." Still I failed to grasp the situation. A week later, I was taking out loose whiting at the fish plant where Nina worked, and noticed her walk in the door. One of her friends took her punchcard, saying, "I'll check you in, Nina."

Then James Bertolino, my *compare*, asked me, "Salve, what's wrong with *comare* Nina? Yesterday she was crossing Main Street, walked right out of the bank and into the traffic without looking. A car almost hit her. The fellow stopped in time and Nina just hurried along. I think there's something wrong, Salve."

I presented all this to Nina and asked her to level with me. "I don't know, Salve," she said. "I feel a certain pressure in my eyes.

They feel as if they have water in them. Salve, I can feel the water running from my eyes now." I couldn't see anything in her eyes.

"You'd better have your eyes checked, tomorrow," I said. I telephoned my daughter-in-law Jean and asked her to make an appointment. The next day we went fishing and Jean took Nina to the local eye doctor. The doctor gave her a test and told her to wear glasses all the time.

Nina never complained about how she felt. I always took it for granted she was well and healthy. She never said anything to her sisters or mother about how she felt. Three months later she called Jean. "I can't see anything with these glasses," she said.

She was fitted with another pair of glasses and told to come back in six months. In the meantime, she went to Dr. Douglas Fiero for a general check-up. He examined her eyes and immediately sent her to Massachusetts General Hospital. A doctor there told her there was some hemorrhaging behind her eyes. She was sent to the Joslin Clinic, which is one of the best hospitals in the world for treating diabetes.

Thus began a long ordeal for Nina and the whole family. For five years we had heartache after heartache as Nina returned time and again for operations in Boston. Dr. Aiello, one of the eye specialists, said she had been hemorrhaging in both eyes, causing her vision to cloud. She was going blind. I cringe to think she went through all this without saying anything to me; she didn't want me worrying at sea.

After dozens of consultations, the doctors said nothing could be done until the bleeding stopped. She went on an extremely strict diet to control her sugar level. We got a bad report when the bleeding stopped. Now Nina could barely see at all. The scar tissue had formed over the lens of her right eye. She couldn't even see light in that eye. She had 20/400 vision in the left eye, at least.

Dr. Aiello and Dr. Sebestyen said Nina needed a series of operations to remove the scar tissue and the cataracts in both eyes. Later, maybe, would come laser treatments and better sight.

The cataracts were removed at the New England Deaconess Hospital, next to the Joslin Clinic. They did both eyes at the same time. I went fishing that day, came into port early and rushed to Boston to join my relatives at Nina's bedside that evening.

It wasn't until the next day that she regained consciousness. Salvatore and I walked into the room. A male orderly was sitting with her. Her eyes were heavily bandaged. The orderly was feeding Nina. Food was dropping on the bed and on her. I held back the tears as I realized how helpless she was. Nina, who was like the Rock of Gibraltar all these years, steadying all the ups and down we had gone through together, was now so helpless.

I put up a cheerful front, chatting away and telling jokes. Then I had to kiss her good-bye and leave for Gloucester. At home, I called my four sons, their wives and children all together for a family conference. "Boys, your mother needs me now," I said. "I can't go fishing anymore. Johnny, you're the captain. Take the boat out with your brothers."

Nina came home and I cared for her. Her eyes remained bandaged. We wouldn't know the result of the operation for another month. I took over all her duties—the food shopping, cooking, cleaning and washing, and paid the bills and kept Nina company as she listened to television day after day.

A nurse was sent to us four times, spending less than fifteen minutes each visit, and sent a bill of $84. I could not afford this much money, so I dismissed her and said I'd take care of Nina. Now I changed the dressings on her eyes and applied the drops daily. Gradually, Nina learned to bathe and dress herself and could get around the house a little without my guidance.

The doctors finally removed the bandages and took a quick look. They rebandaged her eyes and said to keep them on for another week. Every day I had to pull back the bandages and wash her eyes with a special solution and put in drops. During these daily treatments, Nina never said a word. I was getting discouraged. One morning near the end of the week, however, she spoke. "Salve, I can see your white hair and your fat face," said a weak, low voice, "but everything is like picture negatives, dark." Those were the happiest words I had ever heard in my life. I began telephoning everyone in the family.

Nina was far from well. Her vision wasn't good. Sometimes I would find her sobbing quietly. I'd slip her hand into mine. "What is it, Nina?"

"I'm afraid, Salve," she said, my heart almost breaking at her words, "all this darkness."

"Have faith in God," I'd say, "and besides, I'm right here next to you."

As time went by, a different kind of love came to us. I protected her and saw that no harm came to her. I was a big, tough guy on the outside. Now I felt changed.

Finally the day arrived when Dr. Sebestyen announced that Nina was ready for the operation to remove the scar tissue from the left eye. He said the right eye was blind and nothing could be done about it. "Talk it over and let me know," he said.

"When do you want to operate?" I asked right away.

"The sooner the better," he advised. We set a date and went home to tell the rest of the family.

On the ride home, Nina grabbed my hand and said, "Salve, am I going to go through all that darkness again?"

"Nina, it will only be for another month or so in bandages," I said. "And then you'll be able to see good in that left eye again."

The whole family was at the hospital for the third operation. All our friends sent cards and flowers from all over the country. I read them to her and described the pretty flowers. I tried to cheer her and the other patients with jokes and funny stories about fishing.

Then she went home to recuperate slowly. When the bandages came off again, her left eye was blurry but she could see things right in front of her. The doctors said the vision would improve as the eye strengthened. Maybe 20/200 vision was possible, they said, twice as good as before.

Social Security put Nina on disability status, as she was legally blind. Our Blue Cross-Blue Shield Master Plan paid most of the bills. As she got stronger and stronger, I let her help me with the light work in the house and sometimes the cooking. The Massachusetts Society for the Blind sent a blind woman to show her tricks on living without sight. She could light the gas stove by marking the temperature control on the knobs with tape, for example. The woman told me to position the table setting the same way at every meal so Nina would always know that the glass is at two o'clock, and so forth.

This blind woman came four times during our crisis and her words of encouragement were a big help to both of us. "Little by little you'll work out the problems and eventually be almost independent," she said. I told Nina that she'd never have to be independent: she'd always have me.

The boys went fishing and gave me the owner's share. We all got by, though not the way we used to. Nina was getting well now. She was accustomed to walking without guidance.

AN AMBITIOUS FAMILY

In the spring of 1977 I went back to fishing and Nina seemed to be feeling better. All the boys were back aboard the *Linda B*. My son Tommy lived in the first-floor apartment at our 38 Mansfield Street home. When his daughter, Lisa, was born, Tommy started talking about buying a new boat for himself. I would put him off. "You have a boat to fish with your brothers."

"No, I want to be my own captain," he'd argue. But again I rebuffed him. Finally, Tommy was about to buy an old two-man boat called the *Sea Buddy*. The captain refused to sell him the boat because he knew me too well. "Your father would kill me if I sold you this piece of junk," he told Tommy. Less than a year later, this boat sank.

I told Tommy that we'd look around together and find a good boat to buy. With these words of encouragement, he settled down to work with his brothers and meanwhile wrote to boat brokers for prices and pictures.

It was August of 1977, and Nina was feeling much better. She held to her special diet and had regular check-ups with the doctors. Still, I did much of the cooking and wouldn't allow her to do any heavy housework. Confident that Nina was well, I agreed to go to Florida with Tommy and look at a boat he had picked out by mail. I got my granddaughter Nina to stay and sleep with her grandmother. Tommy and I flew to Tarpon Springs on the western coast of Florida.

The broker was a nice fellow and took us to the little fishing community which was a pleasant tourist spot. The boat was a 50-

footer with a V-8 General Motors, 240 hp diesel engine. It was only seven years old and the price was only $38,000. Checking the boat at the pier, Tommy was very eager. I wasn't so convinced. "This boat isn't for you," I said. Dryrot had spread all over the boat. The wood was soft. I probed with a small knife into the wood and showed my son how the blade penetrated so easily.

I was very surprised at this, for it was a relatively new boat. The hot, humid air made it old fast. I told the broker that my son was not interested in this boat and asked to see another. He said the *Sea Prowler*, "a good boat," was for sale in St. Petersburg. We drove over and checked out the 55-foot shrimper. She was freshly painted and looked good. We asked the price. "Forty thousand dollars," said the broker.

Tommy and I talked it over. I said it was too much money for this boat with the same V-8 engine we had seen in Tarpon Springs. There'd be a lot of expense in changing the *Sea Prowler*'s deck around for groundfishing. A new winch, raised rails, and work into the fish hold alone would cost another $10,000. We offered $34,000. The broker said the owners were out of town and would be back in a week. "Let's go home, Tommy," I said.

A week later, the *Sea Prowler* owner agreed to our price by letter. We made arrangements and flew back to Tampa. The boat was hauled out at a drydock and we hired a surveyor to inspect it. The surveyor found a lot of dryrot and worm holes in the the bottom of the hull. "Keep away from this boat," the surveyor told us. Even the broker was surprised by the rot. We took our leave and paid the surveyor and drydock and returned to Gloucester. Tommy told me we could have fixed up the *Sea Prowler*. That's how desperately he wanted a boat.

It was now the end of the summer and Tommy showed me another picture of a boat. This time it was a 75-foot shrimper, similar to the *Pepe*, owned by our cousin Tom Randazza. This latest boat was in Fort Meyers on the west coast of Florida. Tommy pestered me to go to Florida with him, but I had no heart for it. "I'll go myself," Tommy said.

"Salve, go with him," Nina told me. The three trips, including meals and the cost of hauling boats and hiring survey men, cost $2,000. So against my better judgment, we flew to Fort Meyers where the broker showed us the boat. We priced it at $32,000, a damn good price for a boat of this size. The engine was seven years old. I told the owners to take us out for a spin in the harbor so that I could check the performance of the V-8 engine. We had gone a mile out when the engine sputtered and threw a cloud of black smoke overhead. The broker started the engine again and brought us back into the wharf with steam coming out of the exhaust pipe. When we learned that she had water in the oil pan, I said, "Let's go home, Tommy." The broker agreed the boat engine had serious problems and nodded his head. So we flew back to Boston. "I hope you learned your lesson on boats," I lectured.

My daughter-in-law Roseanne, her face white and drawn, met Tommy and me as we arrived home. "Salvatore and Aunt Annie rushed Mommy to the hospital in Boston," she said. Roseanne told us that Nina was washing clothes alone and opened the window to put them out on the clothesline when she ruptured something in her good left eye. She was bending over and the hemorrhaging started, Roseanne said. Nina shouted, but the television was too loud for Roseanne to hear downstairs. Nina picked up the telephone and miraculously dialed the number of her sister Annie, without sight.

Tommy and I rushed to the New England Deaconess Hospital in Boston. Nina's eyes were bandaged and she had been given a sedative to calm her. She didn't hear us, but Salvatore told us the doctor had said the retina of the left eye had detached itself, causing total blindness. The doctor said Nina needed another operation within a week or two. He said we should talk it over. I had already made up my mind. The doctor still wanted me to take Nina home for a couple of days to talk it over.

I came back to the hospital two days later to bring Nina home. I remembered Dr. Sebestyen's warning that if he didn't operate within two weeks, she would be blind for the rest of her life. There was a fifty-fifty chance, he said. I had a lump in my throat, as we drove home in silence. After a little while, I looked at her and noticed she was crying. "What's the matter, Nina?" I asked.

"Salve, I'm going to be blind and I'll never see you or my grandchildren again."

"Stop thinking that way," I told her. "The doctors give you a fifty-fifty chance of seeing again." She shook her head and cried. I cursed myself for not bringing someone else along in the car because I wanted to hug my Nina. "Nina," I yelled. "Listen to me. If I was drowning and a straw floated by me, I'd grab it. Have faith in God and St. Joseph." I knew Nina prayed to St. Joseph every morning. Driving with one hand and squeezing her hand with the other, I said, "Besides, you'll always have me. I'll be your eyes."

I tried to give her courage until we arrived home and called all the family together. We told everyone we were going ahead with the operation. Five days later, a team of five eye specialists worked on her for six hours while my sons and I waited. Dr. Sebestyen finally said everything looked good. "Now let's hope and pray. We've done all we could," he said.

The hospital kept Nina drugged for a week, giving the eye a

chance to get stronger without her moving about. Finally came the day when I could take her home, her eyes still bandaged. The doctors warned me to watch her carefully, because this was her last chance.

The month of September went by and I took her to the Joslin Clinic twice a week for check-ups. Sometimes Jean and Annie came along. All of Nina's *comare* (women friends) and my family came to see her and letters and cards and flowers poured in from everywhere. We had made many friends in our lives.

After three weeks she could see again, but only with thick-lensed glasses. They provided minimal sight. Without the glasses, she was sightless altogether.

NEW FRIENDS

In January of 1978 we took a trip to Satellite Beach, on the east coast of Florida, just twenty miles from Cape Canaveral. Nina's sister Frances had leased a two-bedroom apartment for us at a big condominium development there. We had planned to stay for two months to enjoy the weather and let Nina recuperate. Again, misfortune came.

Nina was wearing new shoes with a leather strap over her foot. The strap raised a blister and turned into a bad infection. I didn't notice the swelling for three days. Nina hadn't complained. Later, I found out why. The doctors said she had lost feeling in her foot because of the diabetes. I was alarmed and took Nina to the Holmes Hospital in Melbourne. She was ordered to soak her foot for three hours every day. They said Nina would require further treatment from Dr. Blackburn. We made an appointment for the following Friday. After more treatments, Nina got better.

In February, I met some very good people who would later become dear friends. While I was shopping in a supermarket, a small, pleasant-looking man with a pretty wife tapped me on the shoulder and said, "I know you. Aren't you from Cleveland, Ohio?"

I laughed. "You're 'way off. I'm from Gloucester, Massachusetts, 'way up north of Boston."

"There's a fellow who looks like you, same looks, same appearance," this man said. "He's a police detective."

"Well, I'm a captain on a commercial fishing boat," I said.

This new friend was Angelo Cavaliere. He invited us to his beautiful home for a drink. As we followed the Cavaliere car, Nina worried. "Salve, they're strangers. They may want to rob us."

"Don't worry, Nina," I assured her. "I'm bigger than him."

Angelo and his wife, Carol, turned out to be fine hosts. Angelo told us that he worked as a bailiff in the Cleveland courts and knew all the politicians—at least the Republican politicians. He had pictures of President Nixon, President Eisenhower, and Nelson Rockefeller on the wall. One picture showed Angelo shaking hands with President Nixon. I didn't say anything about being a lifelong Democrat.

After a relaxing hour of Carol showing Nina and me the house and swimming pool, we departed. I told them to visit us for a good home-cooked meal at our apartment. They did. I cooked steak with all the trimmings and introduced the Cavalieres to Nina's family in Florida.

A week later I got a call from Jean, who said the grandchildren Nina, twelve, and Mary, eight—were coming down to visit us. Nina and I were naturally thrilled at the grandchildren coming. Young Nina and Mary were scheduled on a flight to Orlando, seventy miles away from Satellite Beach. Their mother didn't know, or they would have flown into nearby Melbourne, only six miles from the condo.

Angelo and the husband of Nina's sister dropped by the next day. I fixed both a drink. "I need your help picking up the grandchildren tomorrow," I said. "They're arriving in Orlando and I don't know how to get there. The kids are young and I have to be there to receive them. We'll go in my car."

"We'll see," said Nina's brother-in-law as he sipped his drink.

His answer peeved me. "What kind of answer is that?" Angelo listened to this, drink in hand, saying nothing. After throwing the question at him twice again without an answer, Angelo spoke up. "Salve, I'll take you." Nina's brother-in-law looked at Angelo, gulped his drink and walked out. When he was gone, Angelo said, "He's your relative?" I nodded my head.

Nina came in from sunbathing at the swimming pool. I told her what happened, and she shook her head but was pleased that Angelo would take me to Orlando for the grandchildren.

The next morning, I telephoned Nina's sister. "Where's your husband? I want to talk to him," I said. She said he'd gone rod-and-reel fishing for the day at Cape Canaveral. This reply left me cold. He had refused me an important favor. After all the favors I had done him through the years, I was disgusted with him. I hung up the telephone.

Angelo and Carol used their big van to pick up Nina and me and take us to the airport. The van had bunks to let the children sleep during the seventy-mile trip back to the condominium.

After picking up Nina and Mary, the six of us went shopping in Orlando and ate a fine meal at a restaurant. The Cavalieres invited us all to dinner that evening and introduced their daughter, Nardine, who was about the same age as my granddaughter Nina.

At dinner, I thought how these strangers had helped us, yet my own relatives had turned me down. Thank God for the beautiful relationship we had with the Cavalieres. This incident and others that followed came to a head later that spring. Nina and I were invited to dinner at Nina's cousin's home. Two of Nina's sisters and brothers-in-law were there.

After dinner we played a card game called Thirty-one. We played a ten-cent ante. You could play all evening and not even lose fifty cents. I made a mistake in the course of the game and gave one of my cousins an ace, which allowed him to win. The same brother-in-law who had refused to take me to Orlando called me "stupid."

I flared up against him, shouting, "What are we playing for? Money? Or is this a pastime game?" Recalling all his rude treatment, I cursed him and called him everything in creation, trying to get him to make the first move, for I was fighting mad. In that rage, I could have ripped him apart.

After a lot of shouting and hollering, the family rupture was complete. We haven't talked since. I apologized to my cousins for my outburst at their home, and they understood.

Angelo and Carol took Nina and me shopping many times, for Nina loved to go bargain-hunting for presents for all the grandchildren. She always brought something home for everyone. That May we drove home to Gloucester with my son Joey and his wife and children, who had spent a week with us.

Before the winter was over, however, my in-laws told us about a condominium project in Indian Harbor Beach, on the east coast of Florida. It was across the road from the beach, with a beautiful view of the ocean. You could watch spectacular sunrises from each patio window. Instantly, we liked it. "Let's buy it, Nina. We'll spend the cold-weather months here and go to Gloucester for the summers."

I figured I would soon retire from fishing and at $26,000, this was a bargain. A couple of years later, the asking price for these condos would double. Within weeks, we owned it, but we did not move in right away. We went back to Gloucester for the spring and rented our new house to a local schoolteacher.

FLORIDA

After the winter holidays in 1979, I bought a new Ford LTD and called my friends Angelo and Carol to say we were leaving for Florida right after New Year's Day, 1979. My sister Pauline would accompany us on a trip and spend a month in Florida as our guest. My oldest granddaughter, Theresa, who was seventeen, also would come along and help drive.

We had no furniture in the condo when we arrived there. We had only a guest bedroom set, which Angelo and Carol had bought for us. For four days we all stayed with the Cavalieres while shopping for new furniture. We bought a master bedroom set, a dining room and living room set, plus all the little things that are necessary for house-keeping.

Angelo and Carol were a great help to us. Carol worked all day and helped out at night. We couldn't have met two nicer people. Angelo would give you the shirt off his back. The Cavalieres introduced us to their friends, including Sam Villerie and his wife, Grace, and Lloyd Shapiro and his wife, Sylvia.

Eventually, we moved into our new home, and the days went by fast. All our friends invited each other over for home-cooked meals and to play cards and have drinks. Pauline and Theresa were constant companions to Nina, giving me a chance to get some fresh air and do some sightseeing.

The following spring, just after Nina and I returned to Gloucester, I got a call from Serafino Codinha from Provincetown, who was my son Johnny's uncle by marriage. Serafino said his father-in-law,

Manuel Henriques, wanted to sell his boat, the *Sea Fox*, and retire. Tommy, his father-in-law, Joe ("Turk") Curcuru, and I went to Provincetown and looked at it. It was in good shape. Manuel asked $70,000 for it.

Boats were scarce now because everyone was trying to get into the fishing business. The new 200-mile limit was in effect, and a lot of guys thought they could make a killing. It was a tough time to get a guy to come down on his price for a boat. We haggled over the price for a while, then Manuel agreed to $30,000 cash and another $30,000 to be paid over the next five years. We bought the *Sea Fox*—Tommy, Turk, and I. We became partners by paying $10,000 each and taking out a mortgage on the rest. A corporation was formed, and we named our wives as the officers.

Tommy, Turk, his son Joe and I worked the *Sea Fox* and turned quite a nice profit. We paid off almost $10,000 of the mortgage in the first year. At the end of the year, Tommy became captain. I was ready to go to Florida again.

Taking Peter and Jenny this time, to help with the driving and to be our guests, we arrived at Indian Harbor Beach on New Year's Eve, 1981. The next day we celebrated at Angelo's house. Peter made eight trays of pizza and I cooked fish and shrimp. All my sons and their families visited us during the next three months. Nina loved to see the grandchildren.

During the summer of 1981, I would occasionally go fishing for a day on the *Linda B.* just to get some fresh air. I'd get one of my granddaughters to stay with Nina. I would spend a lot of time repairing nets and building new ones for the boys. I'd keep in touch with them at sea by the radio telephone in my house.

In late August, Nina got an infection on her stomach where she gave herself the injections of insulin. She was hospitalized and had surgery. When she was released from the hospital, she still felt sick and refused to go on walks, preferring to stay home all day. I took her sugar count three times a day and charted it. It went up and down from high peaks to low valleys.

After two weeks she was still not feeling well, so we got an appointment at the Joslin Clinic. The doctor asked if she was keeping to her diet. I explained that she was on the diet but still did not have the energy to walk. The doctor said that Nina had no feeling below her left ankle and that her heart gave some irregular beats. Taking me aside, the doctor explained that Nina's disease was on a rampage through her body, striking at her weakest joints. Her kidneys were slowly deteriorating and she needed immediate attention.

We made arrangements for her to enter the clinic for further treatment. After three days, Nina was transferred to New England

Deaconess for tests and treatments to find out why her blood sugar level was so high and why her left foot was so very cold all the time. They found she had a blocked artery in the groin. It stopped the blood from going to her foot, where now she had a small ulcer; her toes were going black.

At first, the doctors said they were going to cut off the foot above the ankle, but after discovering the blocked artery, they favored a bypass operation to clean out the artery. They operated on her leg, from the groin to the ankle—a thirty-inch gash. My children and I gave her courage; God would help us over this one, too.

Nina noticed me limping whenever I visited her and asked me what had happened. I told her I had fallen and sprained my ankle. The truth was that I had fallen in a hole on the wharf and the sudden jerk of the fall had torn all the cartilage in my knee. Doctors at Addison Gilbert Hospital had operated on my knee the same day the doctors in Boston had operated on Nina.

I was on crutches when Salvatore took me to Boston to see Nina, who was still under the drugs. She didn't recognize me. Salvatore found me a rented room near the hospital so I could visit Nina every day from ten in the morning to eight at night. The room cost $70 a day.

Thanksgiving Day came. It was very blue for me. I was at her side and hoped we could at least have a meal together. She was still under the drugs, and when I called her name, she would only moan, saying that she hurt all over. I stood by helplessly, holding her hand. So this day of thanks went by.

During December Nina recuperated at the hospital and I moved to a $50-a-day room across the street. I'd read the paper to her and tell all kinds of stories to the other two people in the room. I walked with a cane now and my leg was getting stronger every day.

A week before Christmas, the doctors said I could take Nina home and let her heal there. A nurse showed me how to wash and dress Nina's leg.

That Christmas we had a family reunion with all my sons and their wives and children at 38 Mansfield Street. I had arranged one of the sofas in the living room as a bed for Nina so she didn't have to climb the stairs and could be among the visitors. I put a door on the living room to give her privacy and bought some new bedroom furniture for her.

My sons and I gave Nina a Holy Manger with twenty-two figurines. It was over a foot high and imported from Italy. She was very surprised and pleased, for she had always wanted one. In between the holidays we brought her for a check-up. The doctor gave her a clean bill of health and said she was coming along fine. In January, however, the doctors discovered that one of the toes wasn't healing properly. The doctor said the sugar count was going up because of the infection.

Nina started to cry when she heard that one of her toes was going to be amputated. I told her the doctors were very skilled and that with God's will she would keep her whole foot and leg. "So what's a little toe? You won't miss it," I said.

The doctors were afraid of gangrene spreading. Nina was slow in recuperating from this last operation, staying in the hospital three weeks. Every day I was beside her along with my family, giving her courage, for now she was despairing. "Salve, will I ever get out of this hospital?"

"Of course, Nina, as soon as you are well and feeling fine, we will go to Florida and get out of this cold weather."

She came home for two more weeks and then I asked the doctors if she was well enough to go to Florida. The weather there was so warm and comfortable for her. I told the Boston doctors about Dr. Blackburn, the specialist in diabetes in Melbourne.

On February 28, 1982, we flew to Florida. Nina was very frail and pale and had lost a lot of weight. Our friends saw how much Nina had gone through. They would stop and talk to her as she sat sunning herself in a lounge chair I had put in front of the house.

My son and daughter-in-law arrived by car. Johnny flew back immediately because he was worried about the boat and the crew of the *Linda B*. Jean stayed a week and more relatives arrived later.

MY SORROW

We continued to see a lot of Angelo and Carol, and Nina's color returned as she got plenty of sun. She said she was feeling much better. Angelo and Carol would always drop in and ask about Nina's health. They baked a big cake and had a birthday celebration for her on March 7. Now the bond between us was more than friendship. It was love among brothers and sisters. When I was cut off from some of my relatives, I gained a new, very loyal people.

Nina always kidded Angelo about President Nixon, because Angelo didn't want him punished and Nina did. So we all laughed and joked. In April, Joey's wife, Joanne, came to visit with their daughters Christine and Gina. They were to stay ten days. Then my grand-daughters Mary and Nina and a young friend joined us.

I was kept busy washing towels and cooking for all the kids, who let me sit while they washed the dishes. Nina did not feel well now. The grandchildren would go shopping for souvenirs to bring back to Gloucester, and I would put Nina in the lounge chair for the afternoon sun.

I had promised to take the kids to Walt Disney World in Orlando. We planned to on Good Friday, but I didn't want to. Nina said, "Go, Salve. Take them to Disney World. I'll be all right." Early that day I gave Nina her insulin injection, her medication, and her breakfast and called Carol and Nina's cousin Angie, to check in on her while I was gone. Still, it was against my better judgment to go.

We came back late in the afternoon and I began to get supper ready. I asked how her day went and Nina said fine. She asked if I had enjoyed myself. "Nina, my mind was on you the whole day. I didn't want to go," I said.

Easter Sunday arrived, and at seven that morning, Nina said, "Salve, take out my new spring dress. I feel strong enough to go to Mass today. I want to go to communion." We all dressed and went to the nine-thirty Mass at the Holy Name of Jesus Church. We took pictures of ourselves all dressed up in our finery. That afternoon we went to Angelo and Carol's for dinner with lots of friends, and later played cards. Nina enjoyed herself at Thirty-one and talked a lot. I saw this as a good sign.

We went back home and retired by ten o'clock. Around two in the morning, I felt her hand on my face. Instantly, I woke up and asked, "What's the matter?"

"The room is too hot," she said with strained breath.

"But the windows are up," I said.

"I feel hot." She had felt this way in the past, so I wasn't overly concerned. I took her by the hand and led her to the living room couch. I opened the patio door and together we sat there in the fresh breeze from the beach. "This is much better," she whispered.

My granddaughter Nina had woken up and came into the living room and sat with us. I got a blanket and wrapped Nina's shoulders. Nina stroked her granddaughter's hair and then told her to go back to bed. "I'm all right, dear," she said.

Nina and I sat quietly, leaning against each other. After awhile Nina said, "Salve, take me back to bed now. I'll see if I can fall asleep." Two hours later, I was awakened by Nina again. "Quick, Salve, take me to the other room again. It's much too hot for me in here." I settled Nina by the patio again and hurried to wake my granddaughter and have her dress. I was really alarmed now. Nina was hot and perspiring. She was talking gibberish. "Salve, take me to Gloucester . . . bring me home to my children . . . call my sisters."

I was shaking as I slipped into a shirt and put Nina in the car. My granddaughter held her and I drove to Holmes Hospital. Young Nina and I tried to follow Nina as they took her away on a hospital stretcher. We were stopped and told to wait in the lobby.

The clock in the lobby read 4:45 A.M. It was April 19. I telephoned Angelo and Carol and Angie and sent word that Nina was in the hospital.

Finally, a doctor came out, asked for Nina's husband, and told me Nina had suffered a very bad heart attack and was weakened by her other conditions. "I want you to know that her heart stopped, but we revived it," he said. He said the doctor wanted to implant a pacemaker in Nina and thrust a pen and paper at me. I signed the authorization. I was dazed. *Oh God, please help her*, I prayed.

Angelo and Nina's sisters arrived. I asked permission to see my wife. The doctor finally agreed. A nurse led me and young Nina to the top floor and down a long corridor to a big ward with glass partitions. There was Nina, sitting on a bed with her feet dangling over the side, and all hooked up to wires and monitors.

As we entered the room, a great deal of commotion began, and a nurse ran toward us. She led us outside to a conference room, where I met Angelo and the sisters and Angie. I refused to look at her sisters. I thought back to all the months they had refused to call or visit Nina. They were sore at me because of the card-game argument and were taking it out on her. They said I was always home and they couldn't come over to see Nina when I was home. It was a big lie. All these things went through my confused and dazed mind. As we waited, the door opened and a priest followed by a doctor entered the conference room. At that moment I broke down and cried and held my young Nina. I knew my wife was dead.

Father Reese comforted me and took me into the room where Nina lay. The priest said Nina was unconscious but alive when he anointed her with the rites for the sick. "She's now in heaven," he said. I thought how only one day earlier we had gone for Mass on Easter Sunday, and how she was alive and well, and now I broke down sobbing and crying. Angelo and young Nina comforted me.

Carol Cavaliere, Angie, and my granddaughter made arrangements at the local funeral home. We had a wake the following day in Melbourne. The people at the condominium were wonderful. They and Angie sent us sandwiches and cookies and tried to offer comfort.

After the wake, a lot of Angelo's friends, Angie, and most of the people at the condo came to pay their respects and offer sympathy to the family. Angelo and Carol opened their home to all the people, offering drinks, coffee and sandwiches to everyone.

Nina's sisters didn't come to the wake, choosing to drive back to Gloucester instead. The next day, we said a tearful good-bye to Angelo and Carol and flew home to Gloucester with Nina's body on the same plane. My sons had already arranged for a wake and funeral services in Gloucester. Again I had to suffer the agony of another rebuff from Nina's sisters. They sat in another room in the funeral home. Most of the people of Gloucester came to pay their respects, people from every walk of life. There were many cards and flowers.

We buried Nina with my mother and father in the family plot in Calvary Cemetery. A spot is reserved there for me for someday, right next to Nina.

After a month in Gloucester, my granddaughter Theresa and I flew back to the condominium to pick up the car. We spent ten days there and then set out for Gloucester. Angelo suggested that he come along and drive with us inland to Cleveland to meet his sister and friends and spend a week there. We did.

In Gloucester, I returned to fishing with Johnny on the *Linda B.* Johnny was captain, and I tried to forget my sorrow by working as a crew member. I came home at night so tired that I would forget to cook for myself and fall asleep in the easy chair. I was all alone. My back ached. I was sixty five years old and not used to the hard work on deck anymore.

After a few months of this, my body had turned hard and I didn't mind the work anymore. I cooked for the crew and ate while aboard the boat. I couldn't stand eating alone at home.

In August I started having nightmares. Night after night Nina's voice came from downstairs, where I had fixed her a bedroom. She wanted to be helped upstairs. I'd rush downstairs only to find an empty, made-up bed. I thought I was going crazy.

Only the presence of my young granddaughter Lisa and the twins Lena and Laura, in the apartment below me, kept me from going batty. During the days I tried to keep busy mending nets for the boys.

My nightmares continued into the fall. I kept seeing Nina. I told Johnny that I was quitting the boat and going back to Florida. I flew off to the condo, trying desperately to escape the nightmares without telling my sons why I had to leave.

In Florida, it was worse. I saw Nina everywhere—in the living room where she sat, in the bedroom—everywhere. I fell into a rut. I was feeling sorry for myself and sat in an easy chair watching television without paying attention.

Angelo and Carol would often call, but I kept putting them off. I'd make up excuses why I couldn't go out. I neglected to shave, wash, or eat for days at a time. I didn't care. I just wanted to die.

I was watching television one day when a voice came to me. "Salve, you get up out of that chair and get busy with life or you are going to die there."

An idea took hold in my head to write the family history. I got a pen and some writing paper and immediately set out to write down the events of my life and family history.

Pretty soon, I joined a health club with my cousin Charlie Cheverie and started working out three times a week. I took many early morning walks on the beach. Soon I resumed going to dinner and cards at Angelo's house.

To keep busy, I cooked picnics by the swimming pool for the twenty-five families in the condominium complex. When my grandchildren began arriving for visits, I was very busy with them. I went to the pool for a swim every day and began to read the newspapers very carefully, including the *Gloucester Daily Times*, which I had forwarded to me in Florida.

I tried not to be alone. I found that having a lot of people around me was good therapy. Little by little, I eased out of my depression.

A HELPING HAND

Today I live in Florida eight months of the year, coming back to Gloucester in the summer months to visit my children, family, and friends. I also keep busy cutting and designing new nets for the boys. With the repairs, I always keep busy.

Before I close this story, I wish to remind readers that it takes a lot of responsibility to run a boat. Being captain means making the right decisions, catching and selling fish, getting the best prices for them, fighting nature and the elements; and all of this must be done at the right time—or disaster could occur. The crew looks to the captain for their livelihoods for their families. One must ponder all these things. In addition to seeing that the boat operates soundly, the engine and the gear are right, above all, a captain must be a gentleman and not a bastard to his crew.

All I have written is true. I have done writing that I didn't believe I had in me, with my little education. During all this writing, though, it seems as if somebody is holding my hand and the words just flow out. I wrote some poems after Nina died. They are from my heart.

I Walk Alone and Talk to God

With a lone pelican flying above
and a scattering of sandpipers
going neither here nor there
not a soul in sight
and my inner thoughts with me
I like to walk alone at dawn
when everything is silent
feeling the wind on my face
walking the vast white beach
seeing beauty at dawn
the sun rising above the horizon
I see and hear the waves
pounding on the beach
but I fear tomorrow
and then I hear a voice saying to me
I must trust with all my heart
He will work out the dawn
for me for another day.

Looking Through the Window of Time

Looking through the patio window
at the vast ocean before me
of rising wind and lashing rain
of rolling clouds racing by
I dream of past days
of ships and men
with holds loaded full
seeking shelter on distant shores
alas, but now the dream is shattered
and the waning years have passed
and in the shelter of my snug home
I watch the storm clouds racing by.

I fear not the lonely darkness of night
nor the fury tempest of a storm
for I face each tomorrow now
with a shining light within my heart
for I have happy memories now.
                              - *Indian Harbor*, 1982

GLOSSARY

AFT - Back end of boat

BAIL (to) - To dipnet fish from bunt end of seine net

BELLY - Bottom section of the drag net

BLACK SPOT - Shadows of fish, traveling just a few feet below the surface

BOAT FOGHORN - Wooden box bellows, which gives a shrill, piercing sound when the handle is pumped back and forth

BOW - Front section of boat

BROKER - Earning no money for a trip

BUNKER PLATE - A hole on deck, where fish are lowered into the fish hold

BUNT - End section of seine boat, where fish are herded, before being bailed on deck with a dip net

CAULK - To plug, seam, or close

CLEAT - A wooden or metal frame used to tie up ropes or lines

COD END - Aft section of dragnet, where fish are herded together, before being brought aboard the boat

COVERING BOARD - A plank on deck, running alongside the rail, forward and aft, to caulk and waterproof the stanchions

CROSSTREE - T-shaped arm on top of the mast

CROW'S NEST - Shelter for fish spotter on top of crossarm of mast or crosstree

DEPTH RECORDER - Shows chart depth of water below keel; shows contour of ocean floor, including details such as sand, mud, shells, rocky bottoms and hills

DEPTH SOUNDER - Instrument that shows depth from the bottom of the keel to the ocean floor

DIP NET - A round metal hoop net with a long wooden pole attached, capacity for each dip approximately one thousand pounds

DOGFISH - A species of shark, three to five feet in length

DOORS (also OTTERBOARDS) - Rectangular planks of wood and steel construction, used on ocean floor to keep dragnet open as it is being towed

DORY - Small, 16- to 18-foot boat

DORY CRADLE - Wooden device on deck used to lash or hold down a dory on any boat or schooner

DORYMAN - The person who goes out into the dory

DRAGGER - A boat that bottom-fishes with a dragnet on the ocean floor; average length is 40 to 110 feet

DRAGNET - A two-winged, cone-shaped net; average length is 70 to 100 feet.

ENGINE ROOM - Usually in back end of boat

FATHOM - Nautical term to describe depth of water; one fathom equals six feet

FID - A wooden spike used to splice rope

FISH HOLD - Middle section of boat, separating fo'c'sle and engine room; on newer boats, it is at the stern of the boat

FISH SCOPE - Detection instrument used to spot fish on the ocean floor

FLAG BUOYS - Markers attached to fixed or anchored gear, such as trawl line or nets

FO'C'SLE (FORECASTLE) - Crew's quarters; usually below deck in the bow of boat

FOOT ROPE - Bottom sweep rope on drag net

GALLOWS (or GALLAST) - Horseshoe-shaped, galvanized metal frames on draggers, usually on forward starboard and starboard aft sections of boat; used for letting out net and wire cable through big metal hanging block

GORE - Tapering shape cut of a net

GORE LINES - Ropes attached to the side of the net for added strength

GUINEA FLEET - Italian (Sicilian) fishing boats

HAND FOGHORN - Small, hand-held foghorn used in the dory, to warn other boats in vicinity

HANG A NET - To attach net to poly-Dacron, Propylene, or nylon rope

HAUL BACK - To pick up the net from the ocean bottom

HAUL TRAWL - To pick up hook-and-line from ocean bottom

HEAD - Toilet on board boat

HEAD ROPE - Top sweep rope on net

HELMSMAN - One who steers the boat during fishing operations

HOOK - Anchor

JILLSON - Single rope or wire tackle, running overhead, midway from mast to aft gallows frame

KEG - Small wooden barrel, attached to head of seine net, used as a marker in seine fishing

LEATHER THONG CUP - Old-fashioned pump with a cup at one

end of a pole, that goes into a galvanized, three-inch metal pipe used to suck up water, as one pushes it up and down—a back-breaker

LORAN - Modern coastal navigation instrument; used to pinpoint one's position, fix, or bearing

MAIN TACKLE - Wood or metal rope or wire block which cuts down strain of the weight of fish: four-to-one ratio, when cod end with fish is brought on deck

MARINE RADIO - Telephone on boat used to communicate from ship to shore and within the fishing fleet

MARINE RAILWAYS - Wooden cradle machine, used to haul boats out of water for repairs

MARLINSPIKE - Sharp metal spike used to splice wire rope

MEND - To repair nets

PEN BOARDS - Used to build compartments or section off fish in the fish hold

PILOTHOUSE - Captain's quarter; where most of the navigational instruments are stored and operated

PORT - Left side of boat or vessel

PUNT - Small, 10-foot long, open wooden boat

PURSE SEINING - Method of fishing by which huge schools of pelagic fish are surrounded at once; usually mackerel, herring, tuna or pollack

RADAR - Navigational instrument used to pilot vessel in fog

RADIO COMPASS - Early instrument used to get a fix or bearing while navigating

RIGGINGS - Wire rope steplines attached to top of mast, running from starboard rail to port rail and forward peak of bow and stern

RIMRACK - Nets torn apart by rocky areas or wrecks

SCHOOLS OF FISH - Thousands of fish swimming together on surface of water, causing a wake or ripple

SCUPPER HOLE - Hole in the side of lower portion of starboard and port rails, to let trash fish overboard

SEINE BOAT - Usually 42 feet long; carries the seine net and is towed around by the mother ship; operated by twelve men

SEINE BOAT ENGINE (DONKEY ENGINE) - A gasoline-driven power winch used to close the net to trap the fish; known to balk and quit running frequently, thus the term "DONKEY"

SEINE NET - Huge, two-and-one-eighth inch mesh net, 1,200 feet long by 120 feet deep; even larger on newer boats

SHACK - Extra or bonus money

SHAFT LOG - End part of boat, where bronze or Monel metal shaft goes toward inside of boat to the engine

SHARE (to) - To get a certain percentage or get paid from the proceeds of the sale of fish

SITE - A job on a fishing boat

SOUNDING LEAD - A long line (600 feet) with knot markers every 60 feet; used to determine depth of water from below keel of boat to ocean floor; very early instrument

SQUALL LINE - High winds with rain, lasting from fifteen minutes to one hour

STANCHIONS - Wooden ribs attached to starboard and port rails, and inside skin of boat and deck

STARBOARD - Right side of boat or vessel

STERN - Back end or aft part of boat

TOP SQUARE - Upper forward section of drag net

TOW (to) - Commence fishing; dragging a net on the ocean bottom for an average of two to three hours, before hauling back

TRENCHING SITE - Temporary job

WHEEL - Boat propeller

WATER FIRE - Phosphor in water

WINCH - Powerful double-gear drum, used to release and pull up net, gear, and fish from the ocean floor to the surface

WING - Part of the forward drag net section

WIRE CABLE - Steel, five-eighths inch cable; 250 fathoms per drum of cable; paid out at three to one scope on ocean bottom for dragging operations

A boat or ship is always referred to as "she."